BRITISH COLUMBIA CROSS-COUNTRY SKI ROUTES

BRITISH COLUMBIA CROSS-COUNTRY SKI ROUTES

RICHARD T. WRIGHT &
ROCHELLE WRIGHT

Douglas & McIntyre
Vancouver/Toronto

REVISED EDITION

Douglas & McIntyre Ltd.
1615 Venables Street
Vancouver, British Columbia
V5L 2H1

Canadian Cataloguing in Publication Data

Wright, Richard, 1940–
British Columbia cross-country ski routes

First ed. published : Vancouver : Nunaga Pub., 1976.

Includes index.
Bibliography: p.
ISBN 0-88894-394-6

1. Cross-country skiing – British Columbia – Guide-books. 2. Cross-country skiing. 3. Trails – British Columbia – Guide-books. 4. British Columbia – Description and travel – 1950– – Guide-books. I. Wright, Rochelle, 1940– II. Title.
GV854.8.C3W75 1983 796.93′09711 C83-091210-X

Cover photograph by Richard T. Wright
Printed and bound in Canada by D.W. Friesen & Sons

CONTENTS

Thompson-Okanagan Region (continued)

KOOTENAY REGION (4)

SKEENA REGION (6)

OMINECA-PEACE REGION (7)

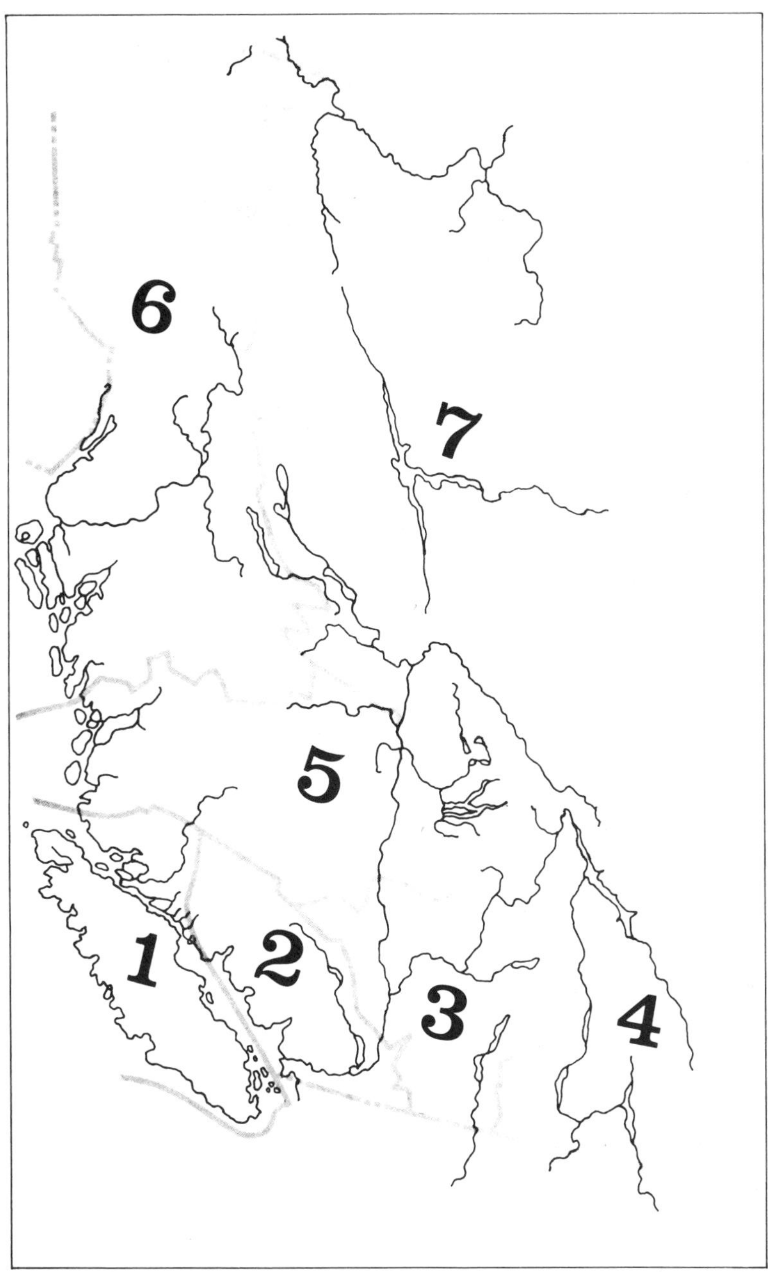

The regions on this map have been adapted from the divisions used in the *British Columbia Recreational Atlas*.

INTRODUCTION

Cross-country skiing is now one of the most popular forms of winter recreation in British Columbia. Whereas ten years ago it was enjoyed by a few Scandinavians and a select group of aficionados, today cross-country skiers far outnumber downhillers in Canada. Many are former alpine skiers who have become disillusioned by costly equipment, expensive lifts, long line-ups and crowded slopes. Others belong to that increasing number of people who prefer a sport geared to individual physical activity.

Cross-country skiing can be a walk in winter, a substitute for jogging, a team race, a test against oneself, or a means of transportation into backcountry. It is one of the best cardio-vascular exercises.

Nordic skiing, as it is sometimes called, falls into three general categories: cross-country skiing on "skinny" skis which are used on track-set or groomed trails by a wide range of skiers from racers and marathoners to Sunday shufflers; backcountry skiing on wider skis by those with an interest in non-tracked and non-groomed trails, many of whom extend their forays into weekend or week-long winter camping trips; and telemarking, a style of mountain skiing based on use of the revived telemark turn and which requires specialized skis for either racing or touring.

The increased interest in cross-country skiing has prompted a similar increase in the development of cross-country trails and touring centres, such as those at 108 Mile Ranch, Mount Washington, Larch Hills, White Lake, Nipika and Whistler. Although some of these now have trail-use fees, the majority offer free recreation. Night skiing is also available in a few locations. Golf courses in many communities now track set the links for winter skiing, and the Ministry of Forests and the Ministry of Lands, Parks and Housing have both increased their trail systems around the province.

This third edition of *Cross-Country Ski Routes* incorporates the many changes and additions made to routes since the first edition was published seven years ago. It addresses what we think of as cross-country skiing, covering areas that have groomed if not track-set trails, or trails that are suitable for skinny skis. Some longer routes, such as the Bowron Lakes, are included as an introduction to backcountry skiing for those who have the necessary winter camping and survival skills.

As before we have made no attempt to turn this into a how-to book since there are many such books currently available. We have, however, provided updated information on, among other things, equipment, safety and first aid.

Finally, we acknowledge the help and support we have had from many people in preparing the three editions of this guide. We welcome further information and suggestions for future revisions.

Richard Thomas Wright
Rochelle Wright
1983

HISTORY

While eastern Canada tells stories of the amazing "Jack Rabbit" Johannsen, and the western States brag about the early mail services of "Snowshoe" Thompson, British Columbia has a delightful tale to relate about the beginning of skiing here. There was a miner called Olaus Jeldness who held a party on Red Mountain near Rossland. The grand finale was the trip down the mountain on the homemade skis he gave to each of his guests. This happened in the 1800s and was probably Canada's first downhill ski race.

The history of cross-country skiing in British Columbia centres around the areas that were settled by Scandinavian immigrants, for wherever small Scandinavian communities grew up, the nearby areas suitable for skiing were quickly found and used for Nordic skiing or ski touring, as cross-country skiing is also known. In some cases skiing was a means of transportation, as well as a recreational and social activity.

According to most accounts, the first ski club in Canada was formed by the miners of Revelstoke in 1891. Ski clubs and communities which had organized skiing by the 1910s and 1920s include Revelstoke, Omineca Club (Burns Lake), Hollyburn, Seymour, Wells, Phoenix Club (Princeton), Viking Club (Vancouver) and Grouse Mountain.

Organized skiing enabled more people to enjoy and participate in the sport and provided opportunities for competition in cross-country races and in ski jumping. Later in the 1940s the addition of mechanical lifts on mountains produced an offshoot of cross-country skiing, called downhill or alpine, which popularized the sport.

More and more British Columbians of non-Scandinavian origins began cross-country skiing in the 1960s, with the numbers picking up momentum into the 1970s. However, the Scandinavians are still prominent in skiing circles, both in local organizations and on national and international levels.

This historic means of winter transportation used by early mail carriers, miners and ski troops, and introduced to British Columbians by early settlers, has evolved to the refined sport we know and enjoy today as cross-country skiing.

TRAIL STANDARDS

To the outdoors person who enjoys cross-country skiing in its purest form, trails are unnecessary and confining. For such a person, part of the value of the recreational experience lies in solitude and the freedom to move and explore where one wishes.

Most skiers, however, recognize the advantages and necessities of trail systems in specific areas. The explosion of interest in this form of skiing has emphasized the need for providing ski areas for large numbers of people near towns and cities, while keeping environmental damage at a minimum. A system of trails can give identity to a specified area as a place to ski and provides more control of safety. For the individual skier, trails help assure a reasonable ski track, enable trip planning according to skiing ability and stamina, reduce anxiety about becoming lost, and provide a way of gauging progress.

It is a difficult, perhaps impossible, task to set down standards for trails in British Columbia, where terrain varies from rugged mountain snowfields through rolling snow-covered hills to grasslands with a light skiff of powder, and where conditions can change from a morning of powder to a melting rain in the afternoon. Generally speaking, the attempt to categorize trails is to provide some differentiation between the easier and more difficult trails, rather than make a precise classification. However, it seems worthwhile at this point to mention some of the criteria used by the Provincial Parks Branch in their classification of touring trails within the park system:

Beginner trail—generally a maximum length of 5 km, maximum grade of 5 percent, a total vertical climb of 50 m to 150 m, and a maximum single climb of 50 m.

Intermediate trail—up to 15 km in length, maximum grade of 12 to 18 percent, a total vertical climb of up to 600 m, and a maximum single climb of 50 m to 75 m.

Advanced trail—up to 30 km a day in length over almost any type of terrain, a total vertical climb of 1500 m and a maximum single climb of 100 m.

An ideal trail should provide for a rhythmic continuous ski motion. It should take advantage of the natural terrain and include points of interest such as scenic vistas, lookouts, natural formations visible in winter, and cabins. Consideration should be given to loop trails where skiers can visit a variety of locations without repetition. These offer a good oppor-

tunity for one-way trails which reduce traffic and hazards. Often hiking trails and logging roads can be utilized.

Those skiers who use and appreciate cross-country trails provided by governments, clubs and individuals might consider writing a note of appreciation and encouragement, or perhaps offer financial support or a helping hand. Every user of a recreational resource should be prepared to put some return back into a sport which gives him or her pleasure.

EQUIPMENT

The choosing of ski equipment might seem to be a formidable chore for the would-be skier confronted by a considerable variety of gear. Individual preferences will vary according to the type of skiing to be done, the degree of flexibility or ruggedness required in a ski, and finances. The four basic pieces of equipment necessary to cross-country skiing are skis, bindings, boots and poles. Generally a good rule is to buy the best equipment you can afford.

Before making any decisions on the purchasing of equipment, we suggest that you do some research to determine what equipment will best suit you:

—Read what the experts have to say about choosing equipment; several books in the Suggested Reading List include this kind of information.
—Talk to experienced cross-country skiers; if you don't know any personally, check with one of the ski clubs.
—Check out at least two ski shops and make sure you are dealing with someone who is a cross-country skier; clerks are usually very knowledgeable and helpful. Probably the best time to seek advice is during weekdays.
—Try renting different types of equipment.
—Take a ski course; many include the rental of skis, giving the participant the double advantage of trying out skis and obtaining advice from the instructor.

As with any apparatus, minimum care of your ski equipment will permit maximum use and efficiency. Following are a few hints about protection, storage and maintenance of cross-country equipment:

—Ski bags help protect skis while travelling, both on public transportation or on the ski rack of your car.
—Keep all ski equipment dry and clean when not in use.
—Stand skis on tails or suspend them horizontally when not in use.
—Store skis in a cool dry area where the temperature is relatively constant.
—Do not block skis together.
—Keep boots protected with a polish or waterproofing compound.
—If boots get wet, stuff with newspaper to keep their shape, and dry slowly away from direct heat.
—Check for cracks or damage to skis and repair if necessary.
—Check that the binding screws are tight so that movement will not make the screw holes larger.
—Check bamboo poles for cracks.

—Check that the basket is secure.
—Repair any weak spots in the pole strap before it breaks.

In addition to skiing equipment the skier must also consider other equipment for trip comfort and safety. What is included will vary with the length and type of trip being undertaken. A small day pack will comfortably carry what is needed for a day's outing; for more extensive trips, a larger pack will be required, while for a short outing close to assistance, a fanny pack around the waist may be enough.

CLOTHING

Dressing suitably for cross-country skiing is a very simple matter. Safety is more important than fashion, so wear practical clothing for winter conditions and don't get caught up in fashion trends. Most people will be able to adapt the clothes they already have, keeping in mind the following general guidelines: clothing should provide good insulation, allow moisture to evaporate, be light, adaptable to changes in weather or activity and allow freedom of movement.

The system of dressing to suit these requirements is called *layering*. This involves wearing several layers of lightweight clothing which can be removed or added easily on the trail. Each layer serves to trap air and body heat. Wet clothes cause heat loss and thereby increase susceptibility to hypothermia. Wool or synthetic polypropylene fabrics are recommended because they retain their insulating quality when wet to a much greater degree than other materials. Generally it is a good idea to remove a layer of clothing when skiing to prevent sweating and to don an extra layer when stopping for a meal or rest.

The following is a list of clothing that can be worn in layers:

—Underclothing. Polypropylene or wool is recommended.
—Pants or knickers. The traditional cross-country costume allows free movement at the knees; jeans or tight pants should be avoided.
—Shirt or sweater
—Jacket. Should be windproof.
—Socks, two pairs, both wool, usually one thin and one heavier pair; if wearing knickers, knicker socks should be worn over the knees.
—Ski boots
—Gaiters, to prevent snow from entering the top of boots
—Mitts or gloves, two pairs; mitts keep hands warmer than gloves, since the smaller surface area means less heat loss.
—Toque. Since the brain is heavily supplied with blood vessels, up to 60 percent of body heat can be lost through an uncovered head—"if your feet are cold, put on a hat."

NUTRITION

Food is the fuel that provides the energy on which our bodies run. We require food to keep our body warm and to supply energy for muscular work. Since cross-country skiing is an activity which requires greater than normal energy to support the increased physical effort, and additional energy to replace heat loss from the exposure to cold, it is obvious that caloric intake must balance these increased needs. Inadequate food intake combined with hard physical activity can cause food exhaustion, characterized by weakness, dizziness and nausea. It also makes a person more susceptible to hypothermia and frostbite.

So to get your ski outing off to a proper start it is important to eat a good supper on the day before the trip and a substantial breakfast that morning. Avoid eating large meals while skiing—frequent small meals and snacks are best— but plan for a big meal at the end of the day. Cold lunches might include whole grain breads, protein accompaniments, fruits, nuts and chocolate. Cooking meals on the trail in winter is easier if you prepare the food in advance and heat it before eating; or if weight is a problem bring freeze-dried foods.

To supplement the planned meals, keep a mixture of high-energy foods handy to eat along the way. Try nuts, dried fruits such as raisins, apricots, dates and figs, and granola, jerky and semi-sweet chocolate. Some people prefer to make up a mixture of several of the above ingredients, commonly called Gorp, and carry a plastic bag of it in their pocket.

Dehydration can be just as critical a problem in winter as in summer. Most people recognize the need for water when it's hot, but during winter activities people also lose a great deal of moisture through respiration and perspiration, and require adequate replacement of fluids as well as electrolytes such as salt.

For liquid refreshment on a day trip it is preferable to bring a hot drink in a thermos or make a hot drink while you are out. Do not eat quantities of snow as too much body energy is required to make up for the cooling effect. Avoid alcohol consumption; it causes body heat loss and can impair judgement.

For longer trips, provision of adequate water supply can be a problem, since generally the skier must carry the water or the fuel to melt ice and snow. However, careful planning of routes can make use of water in streams. If it becomes necessary to provide water by melting ice or snow, keep in mind that it takes less fuel to obtain water from ice than to obtain the same amount of water from snow.

SAFETY & SURVIVAL

Safety in all outdoor winter activities requires special attention because of the harshness of the elements. In cross-country skiing, safety can be even more critical than in general winter activities because of the stress of hard physical activity, the ease of travelling great distances from help, and the potential for exposure. The following pages cover many of the aspects important to the safety of the cross-country skier. Being aware of the problems that might be encountered and being prepared to meet those problems can be the difference between life and death.

Since it is not feasible to provide all the answers regarding safety and survival here, refer to the Suggested Reading List for additional sources. People are well advised to read extensively, since the broader the knowledge one has the better one's resources to face any crisis in life.

Survival in emergency situations in outdoor winter conditions depends on safety precautions and preparedness. There are several recognized rules for outdoor safety which relate to the cross-country experience:

—Begin skiing short distances and gradually work up to longer trips.
—Be in good physical condition before attempting a long or difficult trip.
—Be aware of your own capabilities and limitations.
—Never tour alone. Parties should consist of a minimum of three, except on well-used trails; if someone is injured, one person can go for help and one remain with the injured skier.
—Leave a message with a responsible person indicating where you are going and when you plan to return; report back to that person on your return.
—Carry emergency supplies including food, water, change of clothing, map and compass. (See also the section on equipment, p. 18.)
—Respect the weather and weather forecasts.
—Always be prepared for inclement weather.
—Don't start out on a trip late in the day.
—Turn back early or short of your goal rather than take a chance.
—In case of sudden bad weather, find shelter; make use of natural shelters such as tree wells.
—Keep dry and warm and be alert; use the buddy system to watch each other for signs of fatigue or hypothermia. (See section on hypothermia, p.000.)
—If you are lost, do not panic; sit down and determine whether your chances are better by staying put or walking out.
—If you attempt to walk out, make your route and direction obvious to possible searchers.

PRIORITIES OF SURVIVAL

In the event of making a decision to stay put and wait out a storm or wait for rescue, it is important to understand these priorities necessary to survival:

1. State of mind
2. Air
3. Shelter
4. Water
5. Food

The will to live and the ability to think rationally through a problem without panicking give a person the best possible chance of surviving any situation. The conservation of energy should be a key factor in making decisions. For example, finding shelter in a snow well is much wiser than expending a lot of energy building a snow cave.

Whenever a group of people are out together there should be someone who is designated as the leader and who can carry out the following responsibilities:

—Have a good prior knowledge of the area.
—Ascertain that the trip to be undertaken is not beyond the capability of any participant.
—Be informed of medical problems and allergies of every member of the group.
—Be sure that each member is suitably clothed or equipped.
—Have some knowledge of local weather conditions.
—Proceed at the pace of the slowest participant.
—Keep the group together.
—Be willing to turn back in case of hazardous weather or other problems.
—Monitor the physical conditions of the members of the group.

HYPOTHERMIA

Hypothermia is a condition of the body in which the inner core temperature falls to a level at which the vital organs no longer function effectively: the body loses heat faster than it produces heat. Hypothermia, known to many people as exposure, is a serious condition which will result in death if it is not recognized and treated in its early stages.

Normal body temperature is the result of a balance between heat production and heat loss. The primary sources of heat production are food and muscular activity, which are supplemented by external sources of heat such as the sun, a warm environment or the oral intake of hot fluids. Equilibrium of body heat is maintained by the cooling effects of evaporation, respiration and wind.

The specific factors which lead to hypothermia in the outdoors are cold, wetness, wind and fatigue. Since this combination of conditions is most likely to occur in mountainous terrain, it is vitally important that all cross-country skiers in British Columbia be able to recognize the symptoms of hypothermia and be prepared to implement prevention and treatment. It is surprising to note that most hypothermia accidents occur between –1° and 10° C (30°–50° F).

Symptoms of hypothermia are easily recognizable to anyone who is aware of them. Everyone will already be familiar with the early stage of hypothermia characterized by feeling cold, feeling numb and shivering. As the state of hypothermia increases, the following progression of symptoms will be noted:

1. Uncontrollable shivering.
2. Continued violent shivering; vague slurred speech; memory lapses; incoherence.

A well-built snow cave

3. Muscular rigidity; fumbling hands; frequent stumbling; lurching gait; impaired judgement and reasoning power.
4. Drowsiness; apparent exhaustion and inability to get up after a rest; irrational behaviour; drifting into stupor; decreased pulse and respiration rate.
5. Unconsciousness; reflexes cease to function; erratic pulse.
6. Failure of cardiac and respiratory centres in brain, resulting in death.

Prevention of hypothermia and its lethal sequence of symptoms begins at home with good preparations for the outdoors, and relies on alert responses to any problems that arise on an outing. Home preparation should include provision for adequate clothing, shelter and emergency rations as well as a knowledge of symptoms of hypothermia. Measures to avoid exposure include the following:

1. Dress appropriately.
2. Stay warm and dry:
   —put on rain gear before you get wet;
   —put on extra clothing before you start shivering.

3. Keep rested:
   —travel at the pace of the slowest member of the group;
   —rest frequently.
4. Maintain energy:
   —nibble on trail food such as nuts, dried fruit, jerky or candy.
5. Be alert for signs of fatigue or symptoms of hypothermia in any member of the group.
6. Terminate exposure if you cannot stay warm and dry in existing conditions:
   —give up goal;
   —seek shelter;
   —build a fire;
   —camp or bivouac.

It is the nature of hypothermia that when a person is no longer generating heat, it is impossible for him to rewarm himself; any application of heat must be provided by external sources. When progressive symptoms of hypothermia are recognized, exposure must be terminated and the following treatment begun immediately, even though the victim may deny that he needs help:

1. Get victim out of the wind, rain and cold by providing shelter.
2. Strip off all wet clothes.
3. If mildly impaired: give warm, nonalcoholic drinks and candy or other sweetened food; put into dry clothes and prewarmed sleeping bag. If semiconscious or worse: keep victim awake and give warm drinks as long as conscious; strip and put in prewarmed sleeping bag with another person, also stripped; if double bag, put victim between two stripped donors.
4. Use a rectal thermometer to determine the extent of hypothermia and to measure recovery.
5. Build a fire to warm camp.
6. When the victim has recovered sufficiently, feed him.
7. Make sure the victim is kept warm and dry on trip out, whether he walks or is carried.
8. Get medical help. It is imperative that anyone who has suffered from the effects of hypothermia be taken for a medical checkup as soon as possible, even though the victim seems completely recovered.

FROSTBITE

Frostbite is the freezing of a small amount of body tissue, usually an extremity, and results when the affected part loses heat faster than it can be replaced by the circulating blood. The causes then are really the same as in hypothermia. Extremities should be kept warm, dry and protected from wind; clothing and boots must not be so tight as to interfere with circulation. Alcohol, tobacco, and skin contact with metal objects and gasoline should also be avoided in a cold environment. The areas most commonly affected by frostbite are toes, fingers, nose, ear lobes and cheeks.

As in hypothermia, there is a progression of damage associated with frostbite, and the stage at which it is recognized and arrested will determine the degree of permanent damage. The symptoms of frostbite are pale, white,waxy-looking skin and numbness, prickling sensation or severe pain of the affected area.

Treatment of superficial frostbite is to warm the part with body heat. For example, parts of the face can be warmed by covering with a warm hand, fingers can be warmed in armpits or groin, and toes on a donor's stomach. The area should be kept dry and should not be rubbed with snow. If frostbite is severe, do not try to warm the part but get medical attention as soon as posssible. Since hypothermia is caused by the same factors, a frostbite victim should be carefully monitored for symptoms of hypothermia, and treatment instituted immediately.

The amount of permanent damage sustained by a frostbite victim depends on the severity of the freezing. Warming may leave the area only reddened, with damage similar to a minor burn, but as the degree of injury increases, the victim may be left with a blister, gangrene and the loss of some tissue, or the loss of the affected part. Again, the importance of clothing, equipment, knowledge and vigilance can be crucial to the amount and kind of damage sustained.

WINTER FIRST AID

In addition to hypothermia and frostbite there are a few other conditions requiring first aid, such as blisters and snow blindness, which will be of particular interest to skiers. First, though, it should be stressed that all users of the outdoors should invest some time in a comprehensive first aid course. Skiing on local hills where help is relatively close does not alleviate this responsibility to know first aid. There are a few general precautions to be considered. Always carry identification, including important medical information; special medic alert bracelets can be purchased to carry this information. A good first aid kit is invaluable, but it is equally important to know how to use it. The best first aid kit is one built on your own knowledge and designed for your own specific use; it should include medications and equipment to cope with personal conditions, such as allergies.

If it is necessary to send for help, at least one person should stay with the injured party while another goes for assistance; if the group is large it is best to send two people. It is also important when sending for help in a medical emergency to write down as much as possible, such as the location, details of the extent of the injury, the name of the victim and the emergency contact at home. Where a rescue party is required, contact the RCMP; they will make the decision as to how the search and rescue is to be carried out.

In case of an accident, symptoms should be evaluated and treatment begun in this order:

1. Keep calm.
2. Check whether victim is conscious.
   If unconscious, maintain a clear air passage; check for breathing.
   If not breathing, check circulation.
   If circulation present, restore breathing.
   If circulation absent, restore circulation and breathing.
3. Check for bleeding, and arrest.
4. Evaluate all other injuries; treat in order of severity.
5. Decide whether the victim can be taken to medical help; then proceed to evacuate, or send for help and provide shelter, food and care while awaiting assistance.

BLISTERS

Blisters are generally caused by a rubbing of the skin of the feet against socks. A usual symptom is a sensation of heat. The best prevention is to wear two pairs of wool socks (not too worn) and boots that fit well and are laced firmly. At the first signs of discomfort, remove shoes and socks and cover any reddened, tender areas with moleskin or elastoplast bandage. If a small blister has formed, tape it down; if the blister has become a bubble, use a sterile needle to puncture the blister in two spots, gently press out the fluid, and then tape down firmly. If the affected area is very painful, make donut shapes from the moleskin and apply so that there is less pressure on the blister.

SNOW BLINDNESS

Snow blindness results from the improper protection of the eyes from the brightness of sun reflected on snow. It is characterized by a burning sensation of the eyes, increased tearing and sensitivity to light, headaches and, eventually, loss of vision. Protection of the eyes by wearing dark glasses or snow goggles is the best prevention. Emergency snow goggles can be made by making slits in cardboard or even bark. Treatment of this condition is to bandage the eyes and provide total darkness. Cold compresses may help and aspirin can be taken to help reduce the pain.

AVALANCHES

In British Columbia, more so than in most other parts of Canada, the cross-country skier must be aware of avalanche hazards and should not

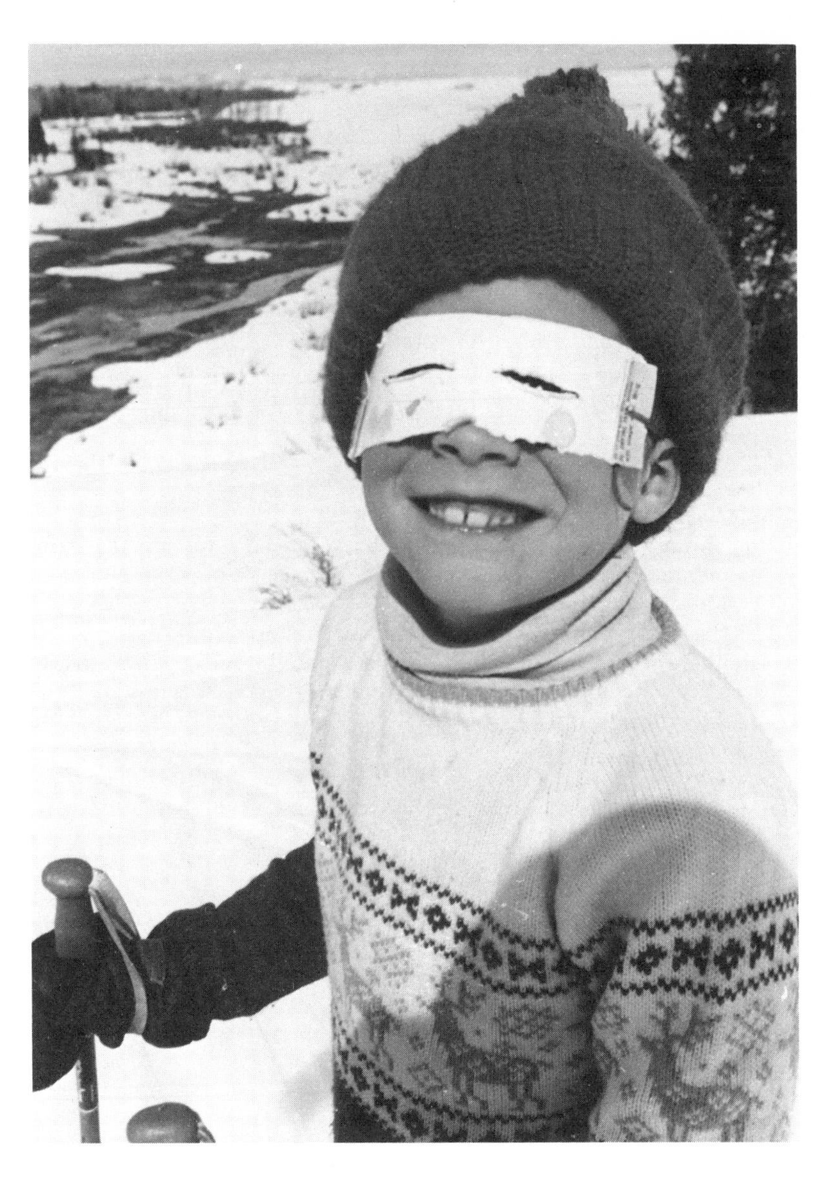

venture into potential danger areas without good knowledge of avalanches. If you have not been trained to read avalanches, stay on the trails. However, you should still be prepared for the possibility of a small avalanche, since under certain conditions almost any slope can slide. The consequences of snow that sloughs off a riverbank or a low trailside ridge can be just as lethal as an avalanche of ice and rock that thunders down a mountainside.

No one can predict with certainty where and when an avalanche will occur, but you should be aware of some predisposing conditions and danger areas. Avalanches are more likely to occur during or just after a snow storm, during and after a wind greater than 24 km/h (15 m.p.h.) or with any considerable temperature change, either up or down. Avoid those areas where pushed over trees indicate that avalanches have occurred before; also stay clear of gullies, open slopes and cornices. Rather, travel across ridges and through valley bottoms or through treed areas on slopes. Before entering an unfamiliar area it is advisable to check with a person who has good knowledge of local terrain and conditions and of any avalanche history.

When it becomes necessary to cross an area prone to avalanches, there are a few precautions to take:

1. Put on mitts, toque and do up jacket.
2. Undo waistband of pack.
3. Remove hands from wrist loops on poles.
4. Put on an avalanche beacon or cord; avalanche cords are red with distance and direction markings and are inexpensive.
5. Cross slope one person at a time.
6. Use the same track as the skier ahead of you.
7. All other members of the group should watch the person cross and, in case they are caught in a slide, note where the victim was last seen.
8. Cross the slope as quickly as possible.

Should you be caught in an avalanche there are several things that can be done to increase your chances of survival:

1. Call out for attention.
2. Try to ski out.
3. Get rid of your pack and poles.
4. Swim to the top; try to grab on to trees, rocks or bushes.
5. As you slow to a stop, create an airspace by putting your hands to your face and pushing the snow away.
6. Try not to panic.
7. Call when you hear rescuers.

If you are a survivor, do the following:

1. Mark the spot where the victim was last seen.
2. Watch for signs of further avalanches.
3. Search for the victim, his avalanche cord, or personal articles; probe with ski poles.
4. Listen for calls from the victim.
5. Send someone for help, but stay at the scene if you are the only survivor; going for help requires not only the time it takes to ski out but

also the time required for searchers to be found and travel back. A victim buried in snow has only a 50-percent chance of survival after the first hour.
6. When the victim is found, check for respiration and if necessary apply mouth-to-mouth artificial respiration. Then treat for shock.

TRAIL ETIQUETTE

Etiquette while skiing, as in any discipline, is mostly a matter of common sense and courtesy. A guidelines are written here for the benefit of novice skiers:

—Try to keep in ski tracks.
—Yield to skiers travelling downhill.
—Slower skiers should step aside to allow faster skiers to pass.
—When skiing in a group do not block the trail.
—The call "track" means clear the trail.
—If you fall, fill in the hole or sitzmark for the next skier.
—Hikers and snowshoers should walk to the side of the trail.
—Dogs should be kept off trails.
—Tobogganers, snowmobilers and skiers should use separate tracks.
—Obtain permission to cross private land.
—Fires should only be lit in emergency situations. For firewood use the lower dead branches from large trees; do not damage live trees.
—Carry all garbage out of ski area.

TRAIL ROUTES

Following are the routes divided into areas denoted on the map on page 7, with a table of contents on pp. 5, 6. An index begins on p. 158.

To be consistent in our measurements, we have given all distances in the metric system. However, some people will be using miles rather than kilometres, especially for driving distances, so here are some formulas for changing from metric to the English system:

Kilometres to miles = km × 0.621
Metres to feet = m × 3.281
Centimetres to inches = cm × 0.4
Hectares to acres = ha × 2.471
Celsius to Fahrenheit = °C × 1.8 + 32

Maps are intended for general reference only. The nature of a book such as this limits scales and topography to approximation. The following international symbols that appear on some of the maps denote level of difficulty: ●Beginner; ■Intermediate; ♦Advanced.

LOWER MAINLAND REGION

The Lower Mainland of British Columbia is not ideal cross-country ski territory. The contours of uninhabited land tend to be too mountainous and steep, and the area's mild climate and changeable weather often make even the usual December to March skiing season uncertain.

In spite of these factors, the Lower Mainland does have areas that can be utilized for cross-country skiing, and has more marked trails than elsewhere in the province. In areas such as Manning Park, the skiing season is longer, perhaps November to April, and even at Cypress Park keen skiers have been able to ski in the summer months. And because more than half of the total population of the province is found here, the trails have the most concentrated use of any in British Columbia.

At the present time, a great deal of discussion is going on among government planners and skiers about further development of both existing and potential areas. What we will do here is give information on currently marked trails and then suggest other areas that are being skied without the need for marked trails.

CYPRESS PROVINCIAL PARK

Level of Difficulty: Beginner, Intermediate, Advanced
Base Elevation: 915 m
Return Length: 0.5 km to 7.1 km
Vertical Drop: 15 m to 355 m
Nearest Community: West Vancouver, 14 km; downtown Vancouver, 26 km
Camping or Accommodations: Limited facilities on Hollyburn Mountain; hotels and motels in West Vancouver and Vancouver
Map: Park brochure available from Ministry of Lands, Parks and Housing, Parks and Outdoor Recreation Division

DIRECTIONS

Cypress Provincial Park is located in the North Shore mountains, and can be reached from Vancouver via the Lions Gate Bridge and west on the Upper Levels Highway, to the signed turnoff onto the 14-km access road into the park.

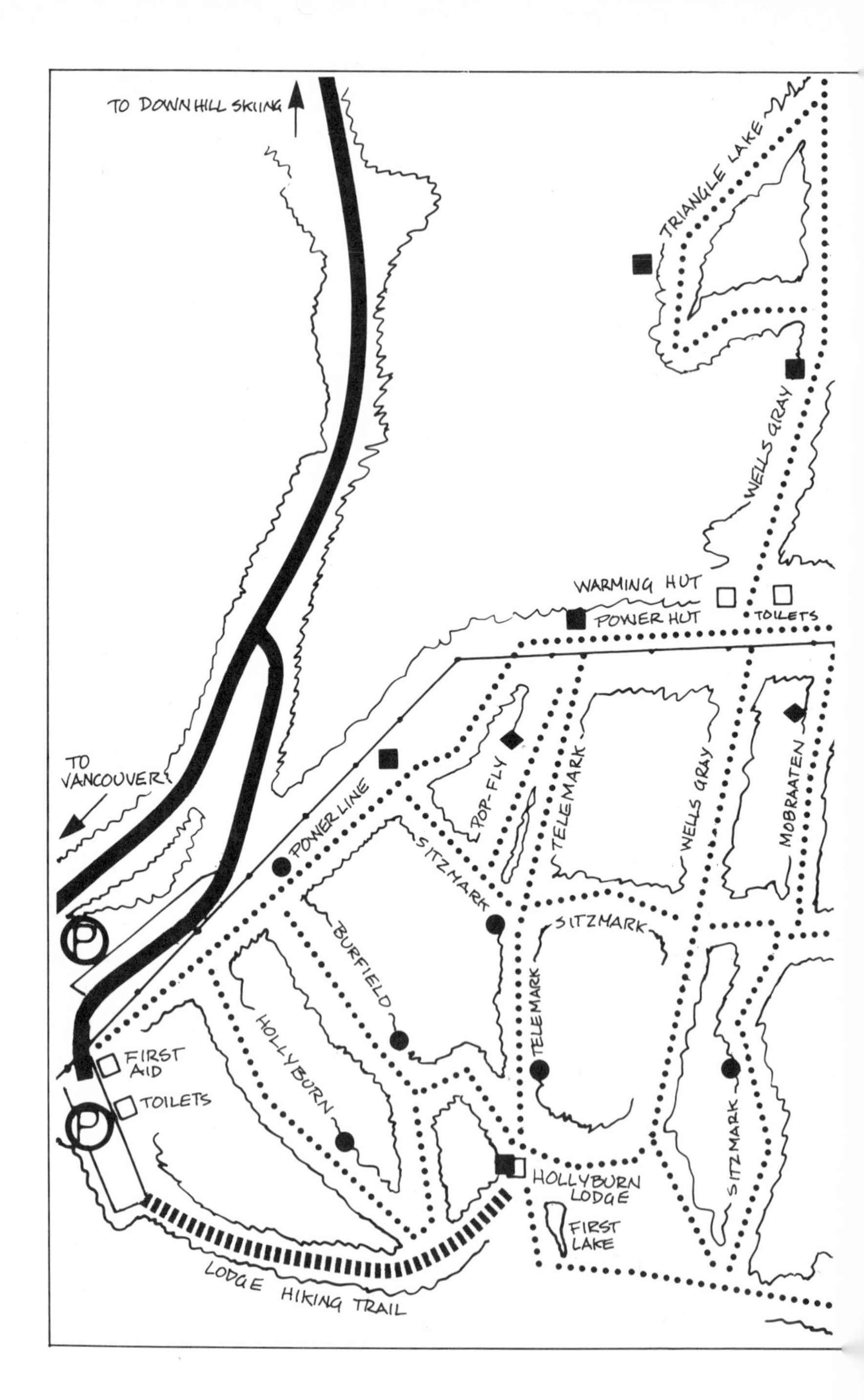

TO DOWNHILL SKIING
TRIANGLE LAKE
WELLS GRAY
WARMING HUT
POWER HUT
TOILETS
TO VANCOUVER
POWER LINE
POP-FLY
TELEMARK
WELLS GRAY
MOBRAATEN
SITZMARK
SITZMARK
BURFIELD
TELEMARK
HOLLYBURN
SITZMARK
FIRST AID
TOILETS
HOLLYBURN LODGE
FIRST LAKE
LODGE HIKING TRAIL

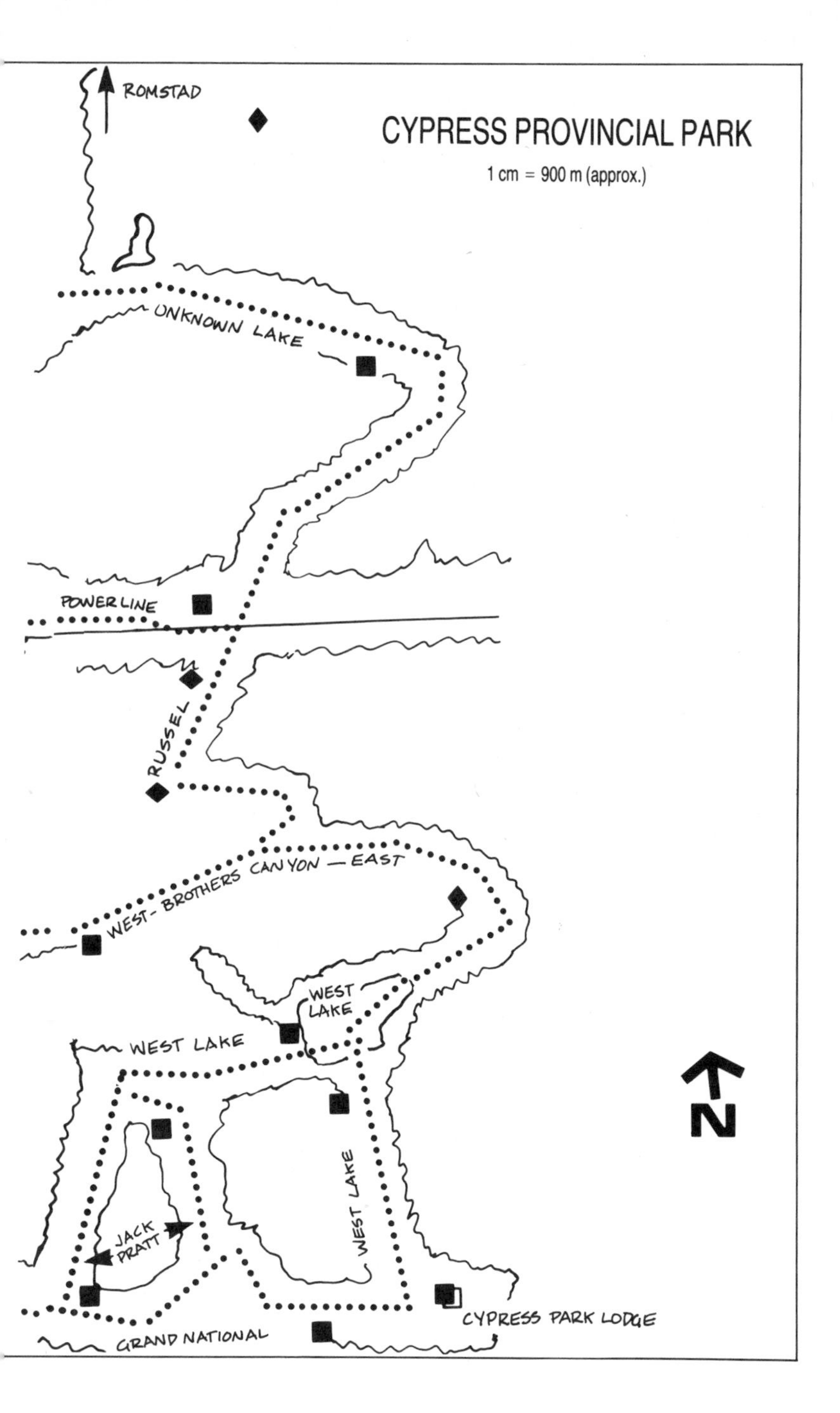

ROMSTAD
CYPRESS PROVINCIAL PARK
1 cm = 900 m (approx.)
UNKNOWN LAKE
POWERLINE
RUSSEL
WEST - BROTHERS CANYON — EAST
WEST LAKE
WEST LAKE
WEST LAKE
JACK PRATT
CYPRESS PARK LODGE
GRAND NATIONAL
N

Signs at the beginning of the access road indicate when chains are advisable or compulsory. Snow tires are not an acceptable substitute when chains are required, and a Parks Branch employee will be on hand to check that vehicles are properly equipped before proceeding up the mountain. Ski and road reports are available throughout the ski season by phoning (604) 926-6007 in Vancouver.

DESCRIPTION

Cross-country ski trails have existed on Hollyburn Mountain for many years, and were used by local skiers long before downhill skiing and lifts became popular. More recently the area was the centre of great controversy involving loggers, developers, recreationists, and municipal and provincial governments. Finally, in 1975, over 2100 ha officially became Cypress Provincial Park. The Provincial Parks Branch has built up a cross-country trail network by utilizing old trails and constructing new ones.

This network is unusual in that there are a large number of interconnected trails within a relatively small area. Though each trail can be completed in less than an hour, many are linked in such a way that longer trips of varying difficulty can be taken.

The present ski touring trails are classified as follows:

Beginner	Return Length	Vertical Drop
Burfield	1.2 km	30 m
Pop-Fly	0.5 km	50 m
Sitzmark	3.6 km	30 m
Unknown Lake	1.9 km	50 m
Triangle Lake	1.6 km	30 m
Telemark	1.7 km	50 m
Intermediate		
Powerline	3.0 km	105 m
Wells Gray	1.9 km	70 m
Wells Gray Extension	2.7 km	100 m
Jack Pratt	0.8 km	30 m
Grand National	1.2 km	110 m
Russel	1.0 km	65 m
Brothers Canyon	2.8 km	80 m
Advanced		
Mobraaten	1.6 km	90 m
Romstad	1.4 km	150 m

Though none of the trails in Cypress really qualifies as a good Beginner trail, they are categorized so that a new skier can at least begin on the easier trails and advance to the more difficult routes as he or she becomes more experienced.

Facilities on the mountain include some outdoor privies, a small building by the parking lot with a room available for skiers, and a warming hut on the Powerline Trail. Also, hot drinks and light meals are available at Hollyburn Lodge, and a coffee shop and some overnight accommodations may be found at Cypress Park Resort.

MOUNT SEYMOUR PROVINCIAL PARK

Level of Difficulty: Beginner, Intermediate
Base Elevation: 1006 m
Return Length: 690 m to 1030 m
Vertical Drop: 20 m to 110 m
Nearest Community: North Vancouver, 13 km; downtown Vancouver, 27 km
Camping or Accommodations: No overnight accommodations on the mountain; hotels and motels in North Vancouver and Vancouver
Map: Park brochure available from Ministry of Lands, Parks and Housing, Parks and Outdoor Recreation Division

DIRECTIONS

Mount Seymour Provincial Park is located on the eastern side of the North Shore mountains, and can be reached from Vancouver via the Second Narrows Bridge, Keith Road in North Vancouver and Mount Seymour Parkway. A paved road leads to the 1000-m level of Mount Seymour.

A sign near the park entrance will indicate when chains are advisable or compulsory. Snow tires are not an acceptable substitute when chains are required. Ski and road reports are available throughout the ski season by phoning (604) 929-2358 or 929-2359 in Vancouver.

A bus service operates between Vancouver and the park during the ski season. For information contact Pacific Coach Lines at (604) 683-2421.

DESCRIPTION

Mount Seymour Provincial Park was established in 1936, shortly after it was proposed by the Alpine Club. The original 274-ha park area has since been expanded to more than 3520 ha.

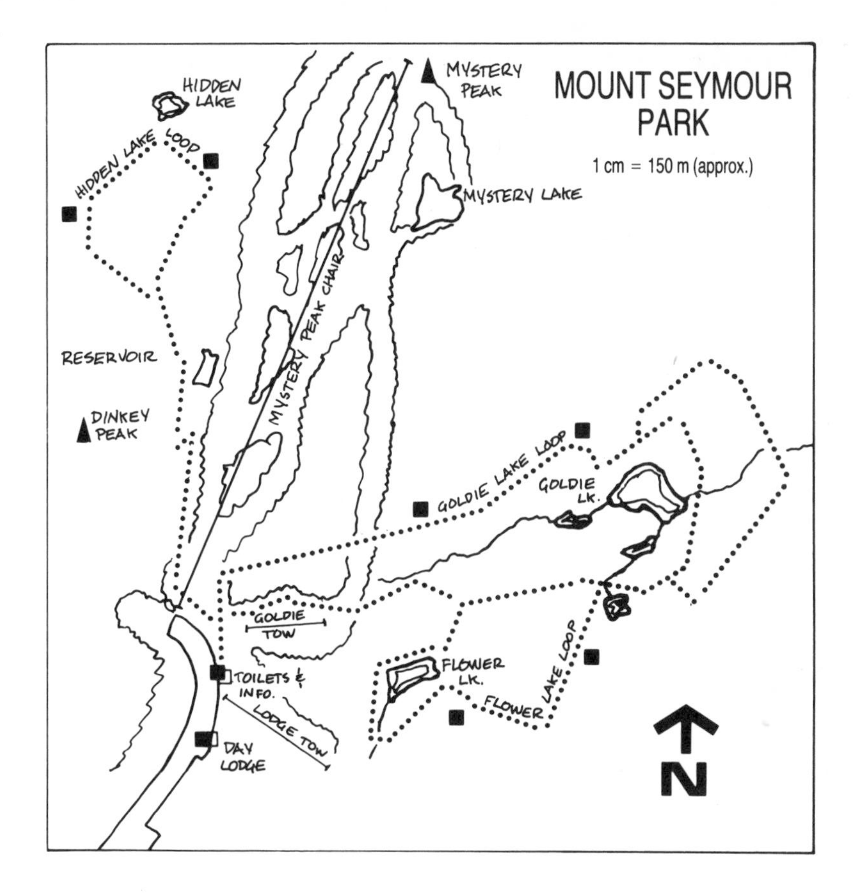

The area has been developed primarily as an alpine ski area, but also provides some routes for the cross-country skier. Ski touring away from the high-use area should never be done alone or by inexperienced skiers as the backcountry is extremely rugged. Notify park personnel if any ski trips are to be taken away from trails or involve an overnight stay on the mountain. Be sure to check in on the return trip.

Trails suitable to cross-country skiing are:

	Return Length	Vertical Drop
Goldie Lake Loop	1030 m	35 m
Flower Lake Loop	690 m	20 m
Hidden Lake Loop	900 m	110 m

Facilities available on the mountain include a cafeteria and a day lodge for indoor picnicking. A First Aid Ski Patrol is in attendance.

BURKE MOUNTAIN

Level of Difficulty: Intermediate, Advanced
Base Elevation: 1000 m at Dennett-Munro Lakes area
Length: 50 to 60 km of trails
Nearest Community: Port Coquitlam, 5 km
Camping or Accommodations: Port Coquitlam and Vancouver

DIRECTIONS

From Port Coquitlam follow Coast Meridian Road and turn right on Harper Drive. Park at the Coquitlam Rod and Gun Club, keeping off the road and away from the club.

DESCRIPTION

Several levels of government are involved with the Burke Mountain area. It is crown land currently under lease to and administered by Coquitlam Parks and Recreation. However, the mountain has been given Regional Park status, and is expected to be eventually administered by the Greater Vancouver Regional District.

There are 50 to 60 km of trails on Burke Mountain, mostly along logging roads that can be used by cross-country skiers. One of the marked trails leads to the summit of Burke Mountain. The snowline is usually about 760 m. Since there has been some conflict in this area between skiers and snowmobilers, it is recommended that skiers use the area indicated on the map in the Dennett-Munro Lakes section. The 6-km common corridor leading to the upper reaches is shared by hikers, skiers and snowmobilers, and courtesy is requested of all users.

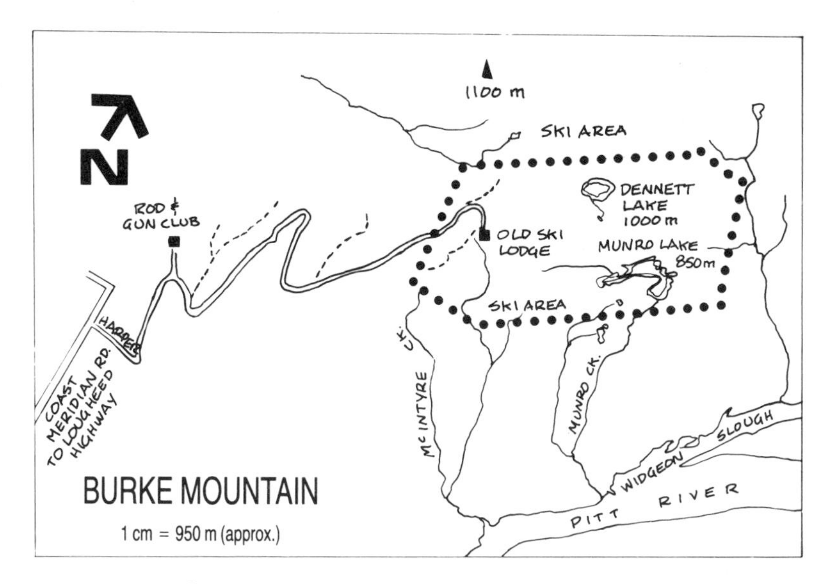

BLUE MOUNTAIN

Base Elevation: 600 m
Nearest Community: Haney, 13 km

DIRECTIONS

Follow Dewdney Trunk Road east from Websters Corners 3.5 km (or 10 km from Haney) and turn north on McNutt Road; continue 3.5 km on McNutt and park to the right in a flat parking area.

DESCRIPTION

Blue Mountain is located north of the Dewdney Trunk Road between Alouette and Stave lakes. There are logging roads into the area, a few of which are still in active use. Blue Mountain Forest is being developed by the Forest Service for winter recreation and for that purpose is divided into two sections: west of the main road for cross-country skiers and the east side for snowmobilers. During the snow season the main road will probably be closed to motorists beyond the 3.5-km parking lot.

Across the road from the parking lot is a small footbridge which crosses a ditch and gives access to toilets. To reach the start of the trail, continue along the main road to a junction, about 0.1 km beyond the parking lot. Turn left onto the side road which goes 0.3 km to a creek and then to a flagged trail going off to the right.

HEMLOCK VALLEY RECREATION AREA

Base Elevation: 900 m
Nearest Community: Harrison Mills, 22 km
Camping or Accommodations: Hemlock Inn on mountain; motels and hotels at Harrison Hot Springs

DIRECTIONS

From Highway 7 at the Sasquatch Inn at Harrison Mills, turn north onto Morris Valley Road. Continue straight up the road following the signs to Hemlock Valley Ski and Recreational Area. After about 8 km, take the left junction and climb another 14 km to the ski area.

DESCRIPTION

This area has been developed as a downhill ski area, complete with three chairs, two rope tows, a ski school and a day lodge with a licensed cafeteria and electrical hookups. There is some cross-country touring and lessons are available. Hemlock snow reports can be obtained by phoning (604) 253-5121 in Vancouver.

MANNING PROVINCIAL PARK

Level of Difficulty: Beginner, Intermediate, Advanced
Base Elevation: 1150 m
Return Length: 4 km to 46 km
Vertical Drop: 30 m to 840 m
Nearest Community: Hope, 68 km west; Princeton, 69 km east
Camping or Accommodations: Winter camping area in park; accommodations at Manning Park Lodge (book well in advance); motels at Hope and Princeton and at east entrance to park
Map: Park brochure available from Ministry of Lands, Parks and Housing, Parks and Outdoor Recreation Division

DIRECTIONS

Manning Park lies 225 km east of Vancouver. Follow Highway 1 to Hope and then Highway 3, the Hope-Princeton highway, to Manning.

Cars should be equipped for winter travel and must have snow tires; chains must also be carried and signs on either end of the Hope-Prince-

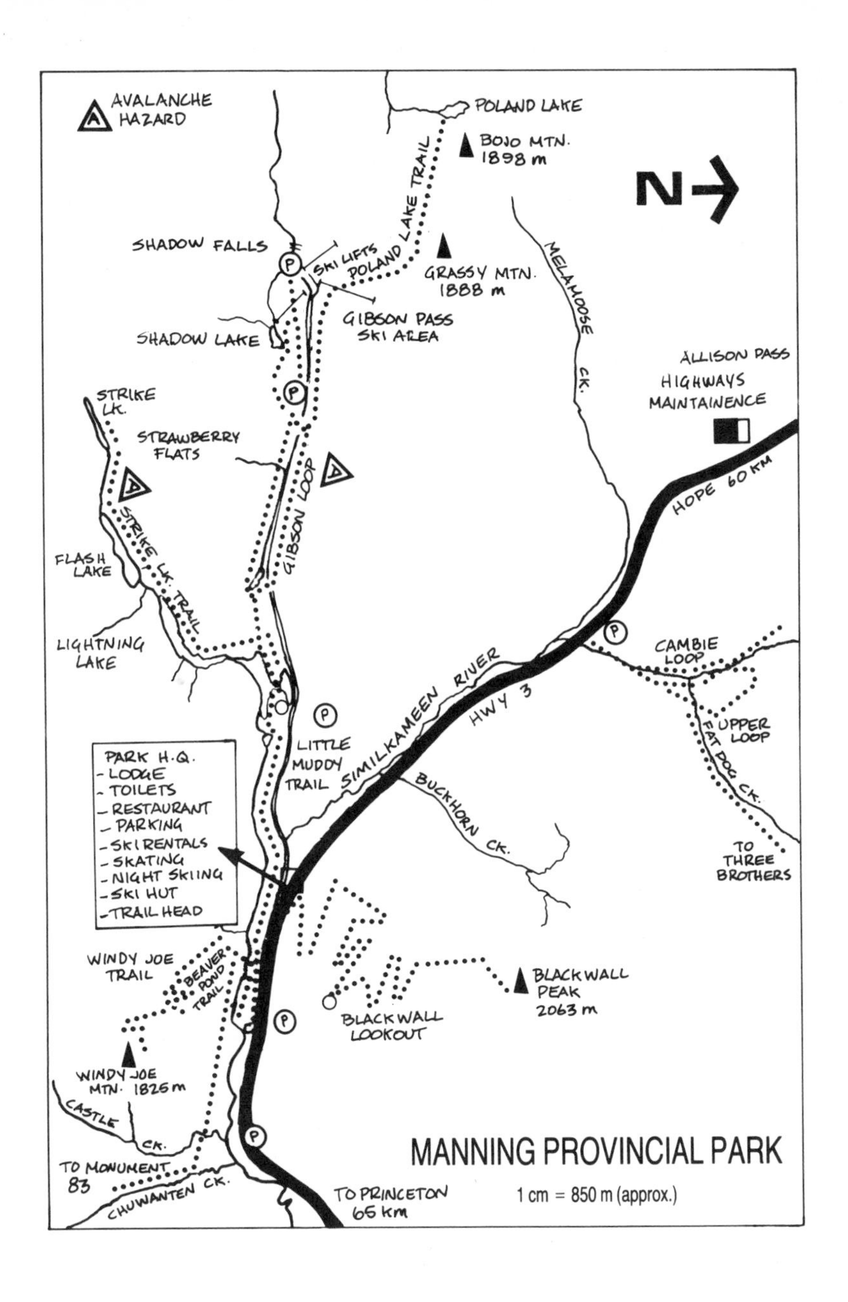
AVALANCHE HAZARD
POLAND LAKE
BOJO MTN. 1898 m
N
POLAND LAKE TRAIL
SHADOW FALLS
SKI LIFTS
GRASSY MTN. 1888 m
MELAMOOSE CK.
GIBSON PASS SKI AREA
SHADOW LAKE
ALLISON PASS HIGHWAYS MAINTAINENCE
STRIKE LK.
STRAWBERRY FLATS
GIBSON LOOP
HOPE 60 KM
STRIKE LK. TRAIL
FLASH LAKE
LIGHTNING LAKE
CAMBIE LOOP
SIMILKAMEEN RIVER
HWY 3
UPPER LOOP
FAT DOG CK.
LITTLE MUDDY TRAIL
PARK H.Q.
- LODGE
- TOILETS
- RESTAURANT
- PARKING
- SKI RENTALS
- SKATING
- NIGHT SKIING
- SKI HUT
- TRAIL HEAD
BUCKHORN CK.
TO THREE BROTHERS
WINDY JOE TRAIL
BEAVER POND TRAIL
BLACKWALL PEAK 2063 m
BLACKWALL LOOKOUT
WINDY JOE MTN. 1825 m
CASTLE CK.
TO MONUMENT 83
CHUWANTEN CK.
TO PRINCETON 65 km
MANNING PROVINCIAL PARK
1 cm = 850 m (approx.)

ton highway will indicate when chains must be put on. Telephone (604) 840-8836 or 840-8822 in Manning Park for ski and road reports during the ski season.

DESCRIPTION

Situated in the Cascade Mountains of southwestern British Columbia, Manning Provincial Park was established in 1941. Encompassing more than 71 200 ha, it has long been a popular area for winter sports. There are facilities for downhill skiing, tobogganing, ice skating and a number of areas that are well suited to cross-country skiing. Most of the trails are suitable for day trips, but there are also alpine areas which make ideal overnight excursions for those with the necessary experience and equipment. Again, it is essential to check in and out with Parks Branch personnel when travelling overnight or off marked trails.

Cross-country trails are groomed and have set tracks in some locations. The skiing season begins a little earlier in Manning than in the coast areas, usually running from about the middle of November until April. There is a short night skiing trail in the vicinity of the lodge.

Facilities at Manning include a coffee shop and dining room and a large modern lodge for accommodations. Ski equipment can be rented from Chris Jaegli Ski Shop.

Wildlife seen around the park in winter includes deer, coyotes, beavers and Canada jays.

LITTLE MUDDY TRAIL

Level of Difficulty: Beginner
Return Length: 5 km
Vertical Drop: 60 m

This trail starts behind the lodge, across the Gibson Pass road near the maintenance building. It follows Little Muddy Creek west towards Lightning Lake. It is usually track-set.

BEAVER PONDS TRAIL

Level of Difficulty: Beginner
Return Length: 4 km
Vertical Drop: 30 m

This trail may be approached from the same point as Little Muddy. It goes east from Manning Park Lodge around the pond famed for several beaver dams. It is usually track-set.

STRAWBERRY FLATS TRAIL

Level of Difficulty: Beginner
Return Length: 4 km
Vertical Drop: 30 m

Access to Strawberry Flats is along the Gibson Pass road from the winter camping parking lot. The flats can be seen from the road. The trail is usually track-set.

CAMBIE LOOP

Level of Difficulty: Beginner to Intermediate
Return Length: 5 km, plus 2 km on the upper loop
Vertical Drop: 100 m, plus 40 m on the upper loop

Park at the gravel pit about 5 km west of Manning Park Lodge. This popular route is used for time trials and marathons and is usually track-set.

STRIKE LAKE TRAIL

Level of Difficulty: Intermediate
Return Length: 19 km
Vertical Drop: 30 m

This trail, which follows a scenic glacier-formed mountain valley, can be reached from the parking lot at Lightning Lake. The route runs through the woods along the west side of Lightning, Flash and Strike lakes, though many skiers follow the lakeshore. Skiers are well advised to either stay off the lakes or keep to the perimeters: the lakes are covered by a buildup of snow rather than ice, and may sometimes only be slush with hard-pack snow on top. There is a beaver meadow between Flash and Strike lakes, and just before Strike Lake a couple of small potential slide areas can be seen.

GIBSON LOOP

Level of Difficulty: Intermediate
Return Length: 7 km
Vertical Drop: 80 m

For easiest access, park at the winter camping parking lot by Strawberry Flats on the Gibson Pass road. The only disadvantage to starting at this point is that the return trip is almost all uphill, as the trail loops around the Gibson Pass road eastward and downhill from here. But the uphill side of the loop is not strenuous to negotiate. Though the road is nearby, the skier is only aware of it for brief intervals.

BLACKWALL LOOKOUT

Level of Difficulty: Advanced
Return Length: 16 km
Vertical Drop: 435 m

Although rated Advanced by Parks Branch, this route is suitable for most skiers. The time and ease of skiing will vary considerably with snow conditions, but where the ascent might take about three hours, the descent can be made in under an hour. On the way up watch for shortcuts between switchbacks. You can enjoy a refreshing drink of snow-cooled water from a creek which surfaces near the road on one of the switchbacks. Once at the lookout there are many areas to explore up towards Blackwall peak and on the alpine meadows. The lookout commands a spectacular view of surrounding mountains and the valley below.

WINDY JOE TRAIL

Level of Difficulty: Advanced
Return Length: 16 km
Vertical Drop: 680 m

Again classified as Advanced by Parks Branch, this trail is suitable for most Intermediate skiers. The route up Windy Joe Mountain follows a fire access road that zigzags to an old fire lookout; it can be reached from the Beaver Ponds Trail. The Mount Frosty Hiking Trail branches off to the south after about 4 km; at 5 km, vegetation changes can be noticed—the forest begins to thin out and alpine slopes become evident. The windswept summit affords a panoramic view of Manning Park mountains.

POLAND LAKE TRAIL

Level of Difficulty: Advanced
Return Length: 16 km
Vertical Drop: 435 m

The Poland Lake route also follows a fire access road up to and then along a ridge to the lake. Car access to the trail head is at Strawberry Flats. The route traverses an old burn area dating back to fires in 1945–47. As well, it passes through a downhill ski run, so watch out for skiers. There is a small park shelter to the south of Poland Lake. A shortcut for this trail is to purchase a one-trip lift ticket on the orange chair for the initial ascent. An alternative return is via the downhill ski area (wearing safety harnesses for the downhill run).

MONUMENT 83

Level of Difficulty: Advanced
Return Length: 46 km
Vertical Drop: 840 m

The fire access road that leads to Monument 83 provides an Advanced trail for cross-country tourers. Access is from the Beaver Ponds Trail, and once on the Monument 83 Trail, keep left at all branches. On the summit at 1982 m stand an old log fire lookout built in the twenties and a new, taller lookout. The monument itself is a border marker between Canada and the United States. The trail is sometimes in poor condition in winter.

DIAMOND HEAD (GARIBALDI PROVINCIAL PARK)

Level of Difficulty: Intermediate to Advanced
Base Elevation: 967 m
Return Length: Red Heather Ridge, 6.5 km; Elfin Lakes, 22.4 km
Vertical Drop: 650 m
Nearest Community: Squamish, 20 km
Camping or Accommodations: Wilderness camping permitted in the park; accommodations available in Squamish area
Map: Park brochure available from Ministry of Lands, Parks and Housing, Parks and Outdoor Recreation Division

DIRECTIONS

Take Highway 99 from Vancouver and follow it about 4 km beyond the Squamish centre turnoff to just north of the Mamquam River. Then follow the logging road— signed Garibaldi (DIAMOND HEAD) on the east side of the highway—for 16 km. Chains are required in winter.

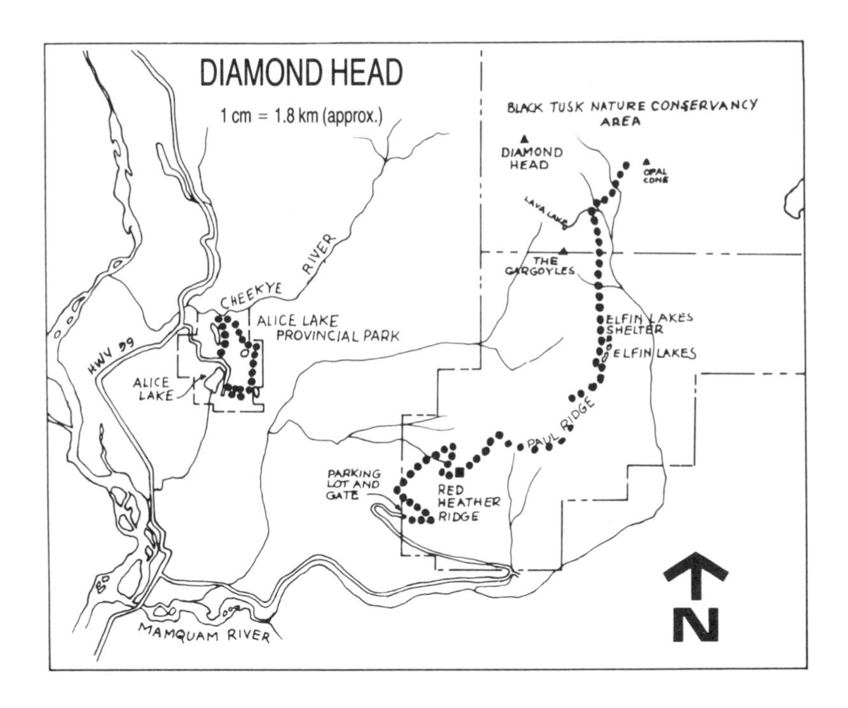

DESCRIPTION

The Diamond Head area forms the southwestern portion of Garibaldi Provincial Park and has been popular with skiers and tourists since 1945, when a family named Brandvold built the Diamond Head Chalet at Elfin Lakes. The chalet is now closed but a shelter at Elfin Lakes provides overnight accommodations for up to thirty people. Overnight skiers into this area should be prepared to snow camp.

Skiing between the parking lot and Red Heather Ridge is suitable for day trips, whereas continuing farther up the trail to Elfin Lakes is more appropriate for overnight tours. The trail is obvious to Red Heather. From there, avoid the avalanche-prone summer trail along Paul Ridge by following the new marked winter trail which is farther south and higher up. The trail is maintained and flagged with orange snowpole markers. The avalanche hazard is posted at base camp when park personnel are in the area. Rescue equipment is located at Red Heather campground and Elfin Lakes. The shelter at Elfin Lakes is intended to serve in winter as a base for further cross-country skiing.

The spectacular scenery is one of the special attractions of skiing in this area.

ALICE LAKE PROVINCIAL PARK

Hiking trails in this 400-ha provincial park, which includes three small lakes, are often used by cross-country skiers when snow cover permits. Perimeter trails encompass Alice Lake and Stump Lake and a 4-km trail connects the two. The access road to the park is 10 km north of Squamish centre.

DAISY LAKE

Level of Difficulty: Beginner to Intermediate
Base Elevation: 400 m
Return Length: 12.6 km
Nearest Community: Whistler Village, 19 km north; Squamish, 34 km south
Camping or Accommodations: Whistler Village and Squamish
Map: Outdoor Recreation Council Map #3, Whistler/Garibaldi Region

DIRECTIONS

Located across from the Daisy Lake Reservoir on Highway 99 south of Whistler.

DESCRIPTION

B.C. Hydro has constructed three loop trails around Shadow and Stanley lakes. A sign at the trail head shows each one, and the trails are marked. No snowmobiles are allowed.

The three loops are:

Sunbeam Lake Trail, Intermediate, 6 km
Shadow Lake Trail, Beginner, 4.8 km
Stanley Lake Trail, Beginner, 1.8 km

BRANDYWINE FALLS PROVINCIAL PARK

A 4-km to 5-km cross-country loop trail is being constructed in Brandywine Falls Provincial Park. From the parking lot on the east side of Highway 99, 40 km north of Squamish, the trail climbs uphill to the north and will eventually loop east and south back to the parking lot. For a winter view of Brandywine Falls, take a side trip around to the right from the parking lot immediately after crossing Brandywine Creek.

CALLAGHAN LAKE

Level of Difficulty: Intermediate
Base Elevation: 550 m
Return Length: 32 km
Vertical Drop: 700 m
Nearest Community: Whistler Village, 15 km
Camping or Accommodations: Winter camping at lake; accommodations in Whistler
Map: Outdoor Recreation Council Map #3, Whistler/Garibaldi Region; N.T.S. 1:50 000, 92J/3 Brandywine

DIRECTIONS

The Callaghan Lake access road is located 45 km north of Squamish or 15 km south of Whistler Village. From Highway 99 watch for a sign on the west side to North Air Mine. Drive along this road to the first junction where you will either turn left or park, depending on snow conditions.

DESCRIPTION

First, a caution: this road is also used by snowmobiles and other all-terrain vehicles; step aside when you hear them coming. The actual length of your ski trip will depend on snow conditions, how far up the road you can drive, and how energetic you are feeling. There are some steep sections and in spring and fall runoff it may be necessary to remove skis and hike so as not to damage ski bases. A short distance from the highway a second junction to the left will be seen. This is a short scenic detour to Alexandra Falls which makes a good rest stop. Back on the main trail, make a left turn at the next junction. You are now approximately halfway to the lake.

As you climb you will see Metal Dome and Powder, or Brandywine, Mountain on the left.

Callaghan Lake is approximately 2 km long and about half a kilometre wide, and is fed by a creek which drains a smaller lake nestled in a bowl of Mount Callaghan only 1 km upstream. This area has been proposed as a major ski resort for many years. The most recent proposal has a Nordic component.

Camping is possible at the lake, but only for the prepared and experienced. The trail continues along the north side of the lake, though it may not be broken. It has been completed to Singing Creek, about halfway along the lake.

Although this trail is classified as Intermediate because of its length, it is suitable for most beginner skiers.

CHEAKAMUS LAKE (GARIBALDI PROVINCIAL PARK)

Level of Difficulty: Intermediate
Base Elevation: 550 m
Return Length: 22 km
Vertical Drop: 300 m
Nearest Community: Whistler Village, 10 km
Camping or Accommodations: Camping at lake; accommodations in Whistler
Map: Park brochure available from Ministry of Lands, Parks and Housing, Parks and Outdoor Recreation Division; *also* Outdoor Recreation Council Map #3, Whistler/Garibaldi Region; N.T.S. 1:50,000, 92G/14 East, Cheakamus River

DIRECTIONS

Follow Highway 99 north of Squamish for 50 km to an access road (signed) on the right just past the "Welcome to Whistler" sign. Park along the access road. Parking is shared with snowmobilers. (Do not park on the highway or your vehicle will be towed away.)

DESCRIPTION

The first 8 km of the winter ski route follow a road that in summer leads to a parking lot. After parking your car, take the first *left* fork, about 450 m up the road. (The right fork is used by snowmobilers.) The trail begins in coastal forest but soon breaks out of the timber into logged areas with a view across the valley. The grade is enough to make you work a little, but it is not a steady climb. After the 8-km mark—the boundary of Garibaldi Park—the trail narrows and runs through an old burn area and then back into the forest. At this point, a trail to the right—signed Helm Lake—heads up Desolation Pass to connect with the Black Tusk Trail. Continuing ahead, in half an hour you should see the lake.

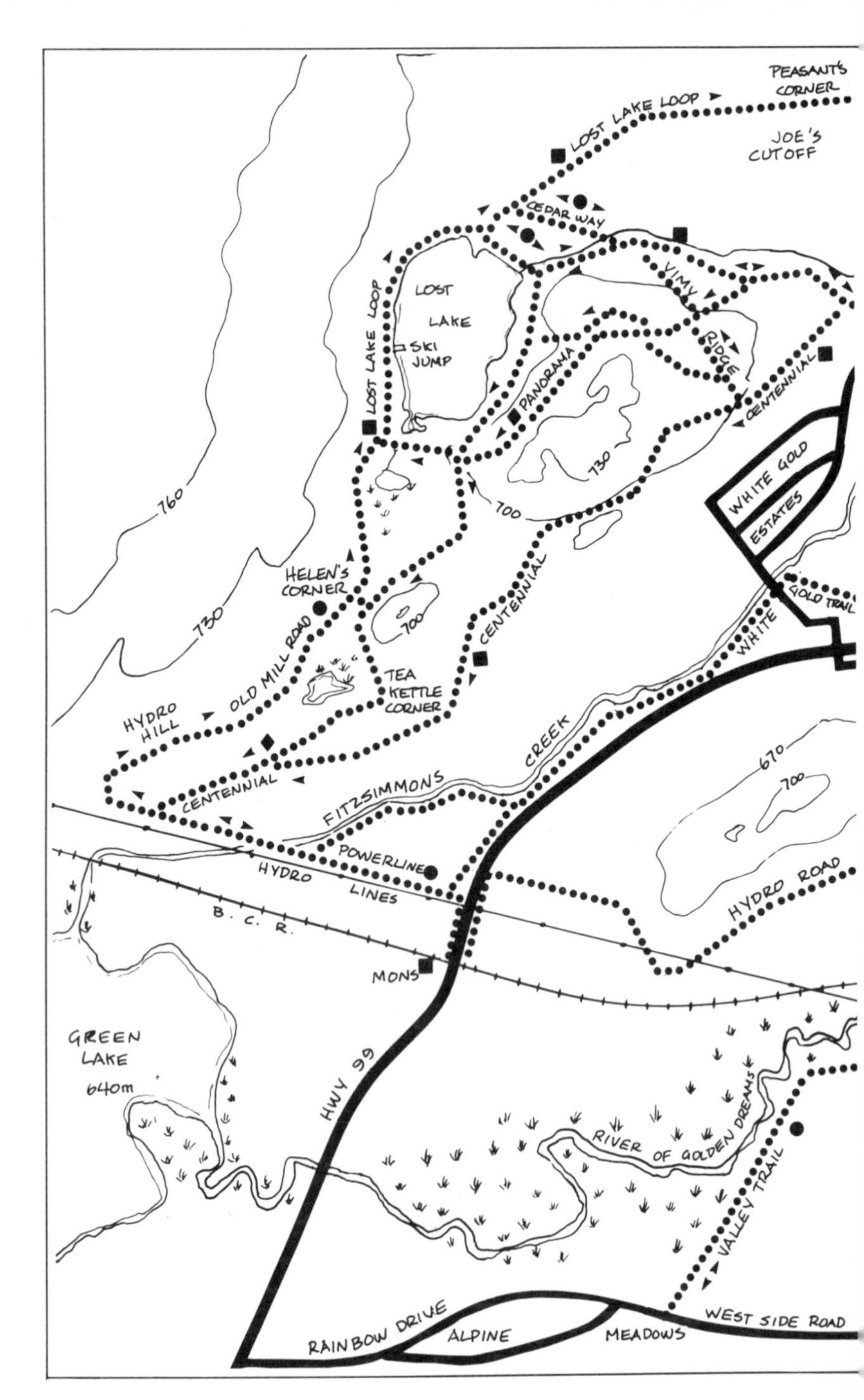
PEASANT'S CORNER
LOST LAKE LOOP
JOE'S CUTOFF
CEDAR WAY
LOST LAKE
SKI JUMP
LOST LAKE LOOP
VIMY RIDGE
PANORAMA
CENTENNIAL
730
700
760
WHITE GOLD ESTATES
HELEN'S CORNER
OLD MILL ROAD
CENTENNIAL
GOLD TRAIL
WHITE
TEA KETTLE CORNER
HYDRO HILL
CREEK
670
FITZSIMMONS
CENTENNIAL
POWERLINE
HYDRO LINES
HYDRO ROAD
B. C. R.
MONS
GREEN LAKE 640m
HWY 99
RIVER OF GOLDEN DREAMS
VALLEY TRAIL
RAINBOW DRIVE
ALPINE
MEADOWS
WEST SIDE ROAD

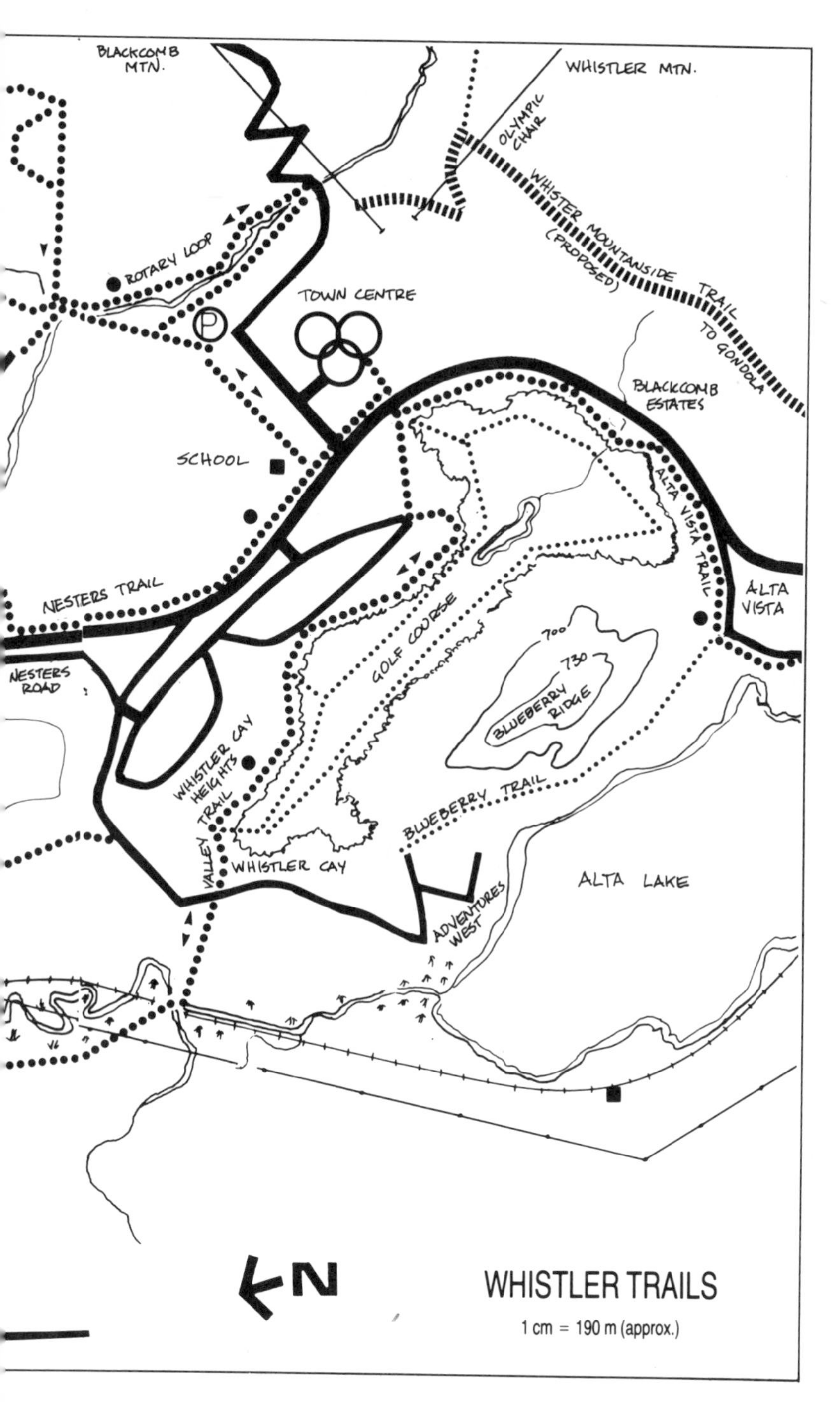
BLACKCOMB MTN.
WHISTLER MTN.
OLYMPIC CHAIR
WHISTER MOUNTAINSIDE TRAIL (PROPOSED)
TRAIL TO GONDOLA
ROTARY LOOP
TOWN CENTRE
P
BLACKCOMB ESTATES
SCHOOL
ALTA VISTA TRAIL
NESTERS TRAIL
ALTA VISTA
GOLF COURSE
700
730
BLUEBERRY RIDGE
NESTERS ROAD
WHISTLER CAY HEIGHTS TRAIL
VALLEY TRAIL
BLUEBERRY TRAIL
WHISTLER CAY
ALTA LAKE
ADVENTURES WEST
N
WHISTLER TRAILS
1 cm = 190 m (approx.)

WHISTLER VILLAGE AREA

Level of Difficulty: Beginner to Intermediate
Base Elevation: 650 m
Camping or Accommodations: Whistler Village
Map: Outdoor Recreation Council Map #3, Whistler/Garibaldi Region; Lost Lake Map from municipality

DIRECTIONS

Whistler Village is 125 km north of Vancouver, approximately a two-hour drive on Highway 99. Traffic is often heavy on weekends and the trip may take longer. Whistler can also be reached by a daily rail service from the B.C. Rail terminal in North Vancouver, which is inexpensive but takes about a half hour longer; a daily bus service; and a private air strip at Squamish. Snow reports for the downhill areas will give some idea of what the valley trails are like. Snow-phone (604) 687-7507 in Vancouver.

DESCRIPTION

Over the past few years the Resort Municipality of Whistler has become a mecca of winter recreation. The opening of Blackcomb Mountain in 1980–81, new runs and lifts on Whistler Mountain, and upgrading and construction of old and new cross-country trails have created a resort unrivalled in North America. Where once there was only a small area at the foot of the Whistler gondola to serve skiers, there is now a completely new village devoted almost entirely to them.

Although Whistler is known primarily as a downhill area, the increased cost of lifts and the lengthening line-ups have turned many former yo-yo skiers towards Nordic. As well as several fine backcountry trails there are now many kilometres of well-maintained cross-country trails. The Alta Lake Sports Club was responsible for developing much of the trail system now found around Lost Lake. In 1982 Lost Lake became a municipal park, and municipal funds were designated for recreation. Trails grew overnight from those around the lake to longer trails that in summer are paved bike paths, connecting various housing areas to the village. These, with the golf course, form the basis of approximately 30 km of track-set trails in the valley. Trails are now available for those who want a full day's skiing, a marathon of 50 km or just a pleasant shuffle into the town centre.

LOST LAKE SYSTEM

Level of Difficulty: Beginner to Intermediate
Return Length: One complete loop, 11 km
Vertical Drop: 50 m

The Lost Lake System is a series of interconnected loops centring around the lake itself. Skiers can vary their route to make a 2-km or longer trail. Access is from a parking lot behind the Whistler fire hall, or from a trail beginning at Myrtle Phillips School.

Beginners will enjoy the easy ski to the lake along the main trail, a former logging road, which follows and crosses Blackcomb Creek. Those who have progressed from walking on skis can continue around the lake, or for a short ski can try the Rotary Loop along Fitzsimmons Creek.

Intermediate skiers and those who have some experience on hills can lengthen their tour by including Hydro Hill on the Mons Loop at the north end of the system. Another interesting loop for those who do not mind hills is the Panorama Trail to Vimy Ridge on the west side.

Many of the trails here were recently improved by the municipality. They are track-set and kept groomed.

NESTERS TRAIL

Level of Difficulty: Beginner
Return Length: 2.5 km or more
Vertical Drop: Nil

Nesters Trail follows the east side of Highway 99 from Myrtle Phillips School to the Bavarian Inn on Nancy Green Drive. It is useful for those wanting a route to the town centre. However, it can be extended by following roads and trails beside Fitzsimmons Creek to the Hydro Road. If you turn east here, you will soon connect with Mons Loop, or the Lost Lake System. If you turn west, across the highway, you will have a good ski through mixed terrain to Lorimer Road and Valley Trail. These latter two extensions can be continued to take you in a loop back to the starting point at the school.

VALLEY TRAIL

Level of Difficulty: Beginner to Intermediate
Return Length: 8 km
Vertical Drop: 50 m

This trail—a paved bike path in summer—is one of the area's newest. It begins at the Recreation Centre in the village, crosses Highway 99, then skirts the golf course past the Whistler Cay subdivision to Lorimer Road. Crossing Lorimer Road it loops around the north end of Alta Lake through the marshes to Alpine Meadows. The trail ends at the south end of Alpine Meadows, at the junction of Rainbow Drive and Westside Road. As an alternative route at Lorimer Road, a branch can be taken to the right to link with the Hydro Road Trail.

HYDRO ROAD TRAIL

Level of Difficulty: Intermediate
Return Length: Lorimer Road to Mons Loop, 4 km
Vertical Drop: 50 m

Although this is not a signed or marked trail for the most part, it links a number of good trail areas and opens up a much longer route incorporating Lost Lake. It begins on Lorimer Road, on a curve part way up the hill, on your left. From here it drops down to skirt the Alta Lake marshes and then climbs a ridge under the power lines. At Highway 99 you will have to remove your skis to cross. After crossing Fitzsimmons Creek you will reach the lower end of the Mons Loop of the Lost Lake system. Turn right here and approximately 5 km later you will leave the system at the fire hall or the school. To reach your starting point, cross to the Recreation Centre and take the Valley Trail back to Lorimer Road.

ALTA VISTA TRAIL

Level of Difficulty: Beginner
Return Length: 2 km
Vertical Drop: Nil

This is another paved bicycle path used for skiing in winter. It begins at the Recreation Centre in the town centre, crosses Highway 99 and then follows the highway and the edge of the golf course south to the Alta Vista area. The trail ends on St. Anton Way.

Those wanting to do some exploring might try the roads and trails that loop through the area between here and Adventures West at the end of Lorimer Road. One such trail cuts high along a heavily wooded ridge overlooking Alta Lake. It is a quiet escape from the bustle of the village.

GOLF COURSE

Level of Difficulty: Beginner
Return Length: 5-km loop
Vertical Drop: 10 m

The Whistler Golf Course is also track-set for cross-country skiing. It can be taken as a circuit of its own or added to the Valley Trail. The golf course is located on the south side of Highway 99.

HURLEY PASS

Level of Difficulty: Intermediate
Base Elevation: 793 m
Return Length: Pass, 26 km; Bralorne, 100 km
Vertical Drop: 640 m
Nearest Community: Pemberton, 32 km
Camping or Accommodations: Accommodations in Pemberton; camping en route

DIRECTIONS

From Pemberton, which is two and a half hours north of Vancouver at the end of Highway 99, take the Pemberton Meadows Road. At 24.7 km turn right across the Lillooet River. The bridge is usually as far as cars can drive in snow season. To reach Hurley Pass continue on this road by wheel if possible, or ski for 6 km, and then turn right up the hill (signed).

DESCRIPTION

The right turn from the valley road puts you onto the Lillooet-Donelly Forest Road. From here the Hurley Pass route is practical for a day's ski, or take a longer overnight journey to the alpine area or to Bralorne. From the valley you begin a climb to the pass, once surveyed as a possible route for the old PGE railway, which was to go up the Pemberton Valley to South Creek and then zigzag up to the pass. As you climb the steep grade you will appreciate why another route was chosen. In 4.8 km you will climb 640 m. That is steep, but you will not have to herringbone all the way; there are some level sections.

The road climbs through a logged-off area and very soon you are treated to a marvellous view of the winter landscape in the valley, and on a clear day you can see jagged peaks and glaciers far to the west. Short-haul roads branch off to either side until after 13 km you reach the summit of Railroad Pass, elevation 1433 m. Should you have the energy to continue, you will soon see Mount Samson glacier on the left. Six km past the height of land a side road goes left; after 7 km another turns right and leads around the northeast side of Chipmunk Mountain; however, to go to Bralorne, keep to the main road and continue to a junction 11 km from the pass. The main road goes straight ahead but Bralorne is reached by a road to the left, after 26 km. For those heading back, there is the 5-km downhill run to look forward to.

McGILLIVRAY PASS

Something a little different for cross-country skiers is offered by Whistler Heli Ski Ltd.: a week's skiing based out of a log lodge at McGillivray Pass which is reached by helicopter. Easy graded side valleys with frozen lakes and high plateaus afford excellent day trips. Tours include visits to old prospectors' cabins and a ski to the former mining town of Bralorne. For further information contact Whistler Heli Ski Ltd., P.O. Box 258, Whistler, B.C. V0N 1B0.

VANCOUVER ISLAND REGION

Vancouver Island offers mountain-top winter recreation in a moderate West Coast climate, in which you can ski one day and skin-dive the next. Even during a mild winter good snow is often found in the higher regions. Although organized winter recreation takes place mainly in the interior of the island, cross-country skiing can be practised anywhere that trails, roads and snow are found. The downhill areas of Forbidden Plateau, Mount Washington, Green Mountain, Mount Arrowsmith and Mount Cain are beginning to develop alternative cross-country trails as the demand increases. Mount Washington has become one of the most important Nordic areas in the province.

MOUNT WASHINGTON

Level of Difficulty: Beginner to Advanced
Base Elevation: 1098 m
Return Length: 2-km to 7-km loops, plus extensions
Nearest Community: Courtenay, 31 km
Camping and Accommodations: Accommodations at the hill and in the Comox Valley
Map: Map of cross-country trails available from ski lodge

DIRECTIONS

The Mount Washington area is 31 km west of Courtenay. Watch for signs in the Comox Valley.

DESCRIPTION

Mount Washington was one of the first downhill areas to develop a complete Nordic program which includes a ski shop, rentals, ski school, ski patrol, snack bar, lunchroom and packed and groomed trails, all for cross-country skiers. There is a day use fee for Nordic trails, and a season ticket is available. There is no fee for children under 12. All trails are groomed and track-set. In March, Mount Washington hosts a 42-km marathon that is part of the B.C. Loppett series. Although other extensions are possible, there are three main trails.

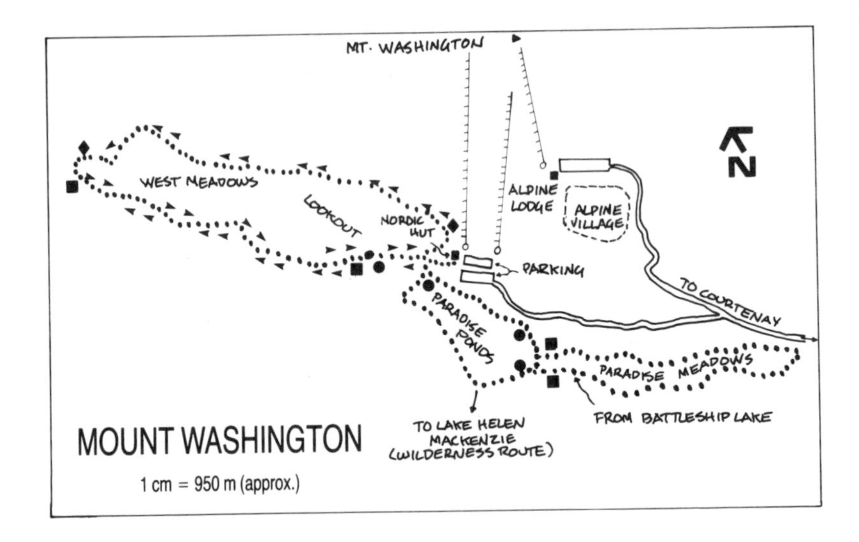

WEST MEADOWS

Level of Difficulty: Beginner to Lookout; Intermediate on south section of loop; Advanced on north section
Return Length: 7.5-km loop

The West Meadows Loop is made up of three sections. Starting at the Nordic Lodge, a Beginner trail goes 2 km to the Lookout. Continuing from there is a 7-km section for intermediate skiers. Both of these have two-way traffic. For advanced skiers a northern section of the loop is one-way and has some steep sections. To travel in the proper direction, the Advanced section should be begun at the lodge. It is about 3 km in length for a total loop of 7.5 km. West Meadows ski trails are groomed but not patrolled.

PARADISE PONDS

Level of Difficulty: Beginner
Return Length: 3-km loop

Paradise Ponds Trail is groomed and patrolled. It is reached from the Nordic Lodge. At the far end of the loop the Paradise Meadows Trail begins, an Intermediate trail. From the Ponds Trail there is an extension to Lake Helen MacKenzie, which is not track-set or patrolled.

PARADISE MEADOWS

Level of Difficulty: Intermediate
Return Length: 6.5-km loop

Paradise Meadows is an extension of the Paradise Ponds Trail, for a total loop of 9.5 km. It is groomed and patrolled. Two other trails extend from the loop, one to Battleship Lake and another called the Marathon extension. Neither is track-set or patrolled.

GREEN MOUNTAIN LOGGING ROADS

Nearest Community: Nanaimo, 56 km

DIRECTIONS

From Highway 1 running between Victoria and Nanaimo, turn east on the side road just north of the Nanaimo River bridge at Cassidy. Go 13 km along the side road, through the Crown Zellerbach gate, and then continue along the main logging road about another 14 km.

DESCRIPTION

The Green Mountain logging roads fan out in several directions following the many tributaries of the Nanaimo River. This is a popular area with local cross-country skiers.

ARROWSMITH MOUNTAIN SKI AREA

Level of Difficulty: Beginner to Intermediate
Base Elevation: 975 m
Return Length: 3.2 km and 4.8 km
Vertical Drop: 76 m
Nearest Community: Port Alberni, 32 km
Camping or Accommodations: Camping allowed anywhere within the regional park; hotels and motels in Port Alberni

DIRECTIONS

Go east on Highway 4 from Parksville approximately 40 km; turn south on side road (signed) and continue another 22 km to ski lodge.

DESCRIPTION

The terrain through which the ski trails pass is heavily wooded at lower levels. Higher elevations allow for fine vistas and are generally alpine in nature. There are deer and a variety of birds in the area.

A cafeteria at the lodge serves meals. Instruction and rentals are also available. Other winter activities include snowmobiling, snowshoeing, tobogganing and camping.

STRATHCONA PROVINCIAL PARK

This very large provincial park located approximately in the centre of Vancouver Island includes three nature conservancy areas. It is basically a wilderness park, and access is quite limited. There are two access points of interest to cross-country skiers, however. The Forbidden Plateau access is completely separate from the road into Buttle Lake.

The ski season is generally from December through March.

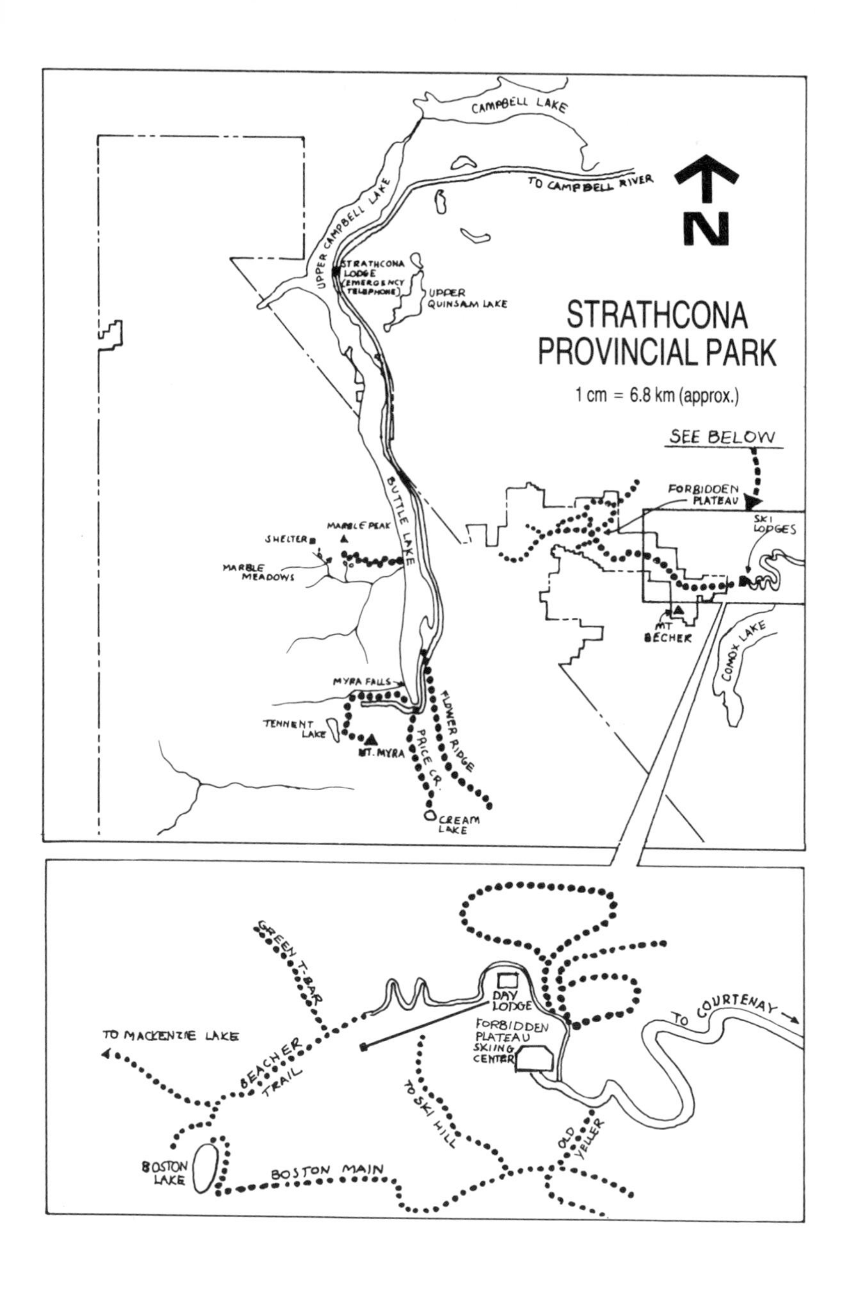

CAMPBELL LAKE
TO CAMPBELL RIVER
N
UPPER CAMPBELL LAKE
STRATHCONA LODGE (EMERGENCY TELEPHONE)
UPPER QUINSAM LAKE
STRATHCONA PROVINCIAL PARK
1 cm = 6.8 km (approx.)
SEE BELOW
FORBIDDEN PLATEAU
SKI LODGES
BUTTLE LAKE
MARBLE PEAK
SHELTER
MARBLE MEADOWS
MT BECHER
COMOX LAKE
MYRA FALLS
TENNENT LAKE
MT. MYRA
PRICE CR.
FLOWER RIDGE
CREAM LAKE
GREEN T-BAR
DAY LODGE
TO COURTENAY
TO MACKENZIE LAKE
BEACHER TRAIL
FORBIDDEN PLATEAU SKIING CENTER
TO SKI HILL
OLD YELLER
BOSTON LAKE
BOSTON MAIN

FORBIDDEN PLATEAU TRAILS

Level of Difficulty: Beginner, Intermediate, Advanced
Nearest Community: Courtenay, 19 km
Camping or Accommodations: Forbidden Plateau Lodge and Courtenay
Map: Photocopied map outlining cross-country trails available from Forbidden Plateau Lodge

DIRECTIONS

Follow Highway 1 to Courtenay and then look for road signs to Forbidden Plateau on a back road which leads west up to the ski area.

DESCRIPTION

A network of marked trails has been developed between Forbidden Plateau Lodge and Mount Becher. They utilize old logging roads and can be followed different ways to make varying lengths of ski tours. One example of the routes available is the Boston Main, an Intermediate trail of about 7 km return length. The vertical drop of the route is about 200 m, and it takes approximately three hours to cover. The landscape is very scenic through the Boston Canyon, overlooking Comox Lake, Comox Valley and the Strait of Georgia.

Forbidden Plateau Lodge was first built in 1928 and has catered to many skiers over the years. Cross-country rentals are available there, although children's sizes are limited, and lessons are offered, including cross-country tours and overnight camping trips. Downhill skiing and snowshoeing are also available. The lodge has a coffee shop and a dining room; accommodations include breakfast and dinner, and are based on double occupancy or dorm style.

Farther west on Forbidden Plateau is alpine country which provides good cross-country touring. Since trails are not marked it is important to be equipped with topographical maps of the area.

CREAM LAKE TRAIL

Return Length: 19 km
Nearest Community: Campbell River, 84 km
Camping or Accommodations: Lodges on Upper and Lower Campbell lakes; Campbell River and Gold River
Map: Park brochure available from Ministry of Lands, Parks and Housing, Parks and Outdoor Recreation Division; large-scale topographical maps available from Ministry of Environment, Survey and Resource Mapping Branch

DIRECTIONS

Take Highway 28 from Campbell River 48 km to Buttle Lake Road and go south 35 km to the end of the lake.

DESCRIPTION

The trail leads south from the south end of Buttle Lake following Thelwood Creek, and then Prince Creek to Cream Lake.

STRATHCONA PARK LODGE LOGGING ROADS

About 16 km of old logging roads in the vicinity of Strathcona Lodge are used for ski touring. They range from flat to quite steep, twisty trails. Skiing on these roads, however, is dependent on a good snowfall.

Accommodations are available at Strathcona Lodge for tourers who wish to make it a base for day trips. It is advisable to make reservations at least a week in advance. The lodge also has a 366-m rope tow ski run and lakeside sauna and shower facilities.

CARIBOO REGION

Like the Thompson-Okanagan Region, the Cariboo is part of the interior plateau of British Columbia, and has similar contours which make it excellent terrain for cross-country skiers. Almost all of the Cariboo that is accessible by road is good cross-country territory, as long as there is enough snow around. In a good year the rolling hills and open benches may be covered in snow from November to March.

CIRCLE H NORDIC TRAILS

Level of Difficulty: Beginner to Advanced
Length: 82 km total
Nearest Community: Clinton, 40 km
Camping or Accommodations: Circle H Lodge and Clinton
Map: Available from Circle H Lodge, P.O. Box 7, Jesmond, B.C. V0K 1K0

DIRECTIONS

Trails are located around Circle H Lodge, which is on Jesmond Road and reached from Clinton on Highway 97.

DESCRIPTION

Many of these trails are summer horse trails and were not originally designed for skiing. Some are so steep that snow machines cannot groom them, so are suitable only for advanced skiers. Others are excellent for beginners and intermediates in good snow years.

FLYING U TRAILS

Level of Difficulty: Beginner to Advanced
Base Elevation: 1100 m
Length: 85 km total
Nearest Community: 70 Mile House, 10 km
Camping or Accommodations: Flying U Ranch and 70 Mile House
Map: Trail map available from Flying U Ranch, P.O. Box 69, 70 Mile House, B.C. V0K 2E0

DIRECTIONS

Flying U trails are reached from Highway 97 at 70 Mile House. They all radiate from the ranch.

DESCRIPTION

The Flying U Ranch has one of the longest systems of trails in the province. Most are groomed. They range from short Beginner trails, such as 3-km Grouse, 3.5-km Circle and 2-km Golf Course, to the Advanced 5-km Gymkhana Trail. Intermediate trails include Little Horse, 11-km Eden and the 7-km Loop Trail. Skiers are requested to sign the lodge guest book to indicate which trail they will be skiing and the approximate time of return, and to check in when they return.

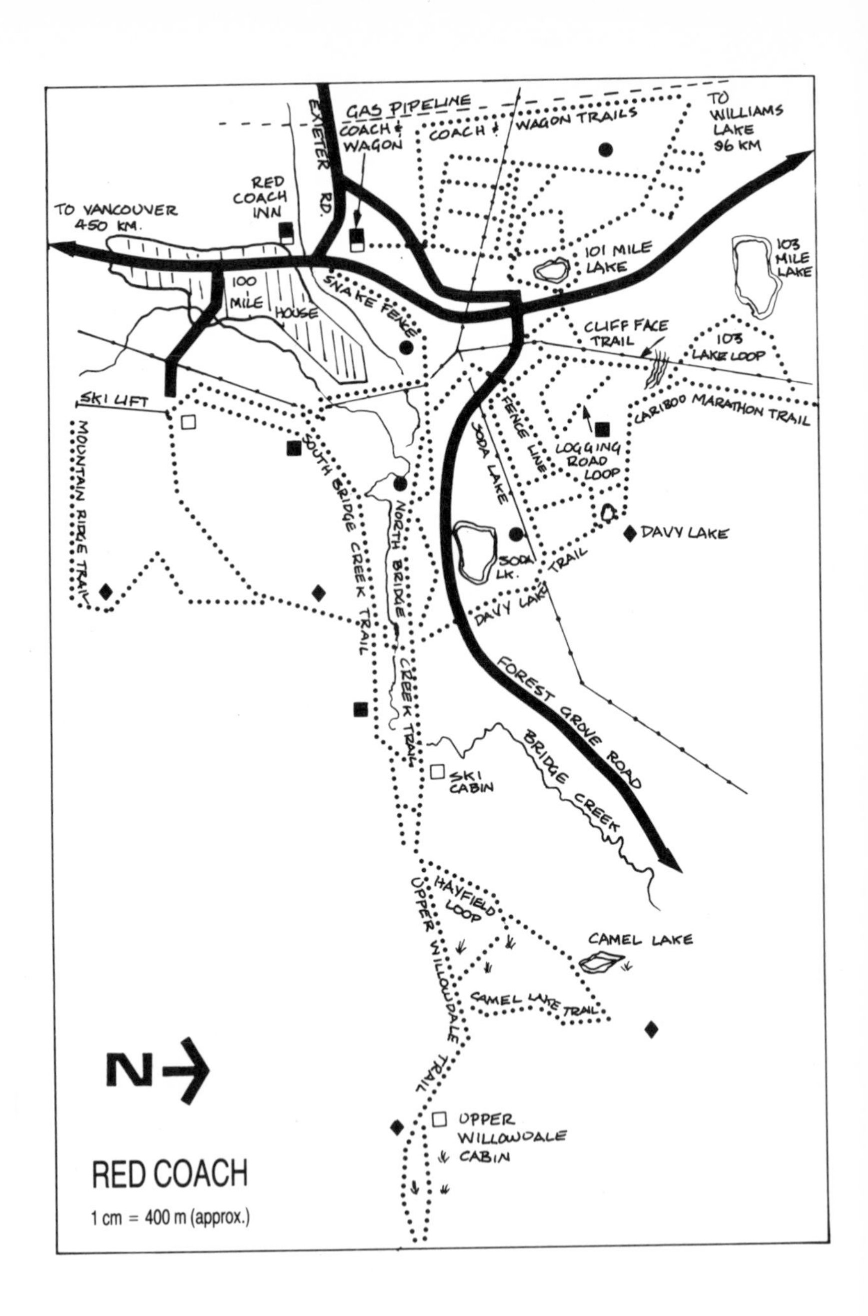
GAS PIPELINE
EXETER RD.
COACH & WAGON
COACH & WAGON TRAILS
TO WILLIAMS LAKE 96 KM
RED COACH INN
TO VANCOUVER 450 KM.
101 MILE LAKE
103 MILE LAKE
100 MILE HOUSE
SNAKE FENCE
CLIFF FACE TRAIL
103 LAKE LOOP
CARIBOO MARATHON TRAIL
SKI LIFT
MOUNTAIN RIDGE TRAIL
SOUTH BRIDGE CREEK TRAIL
NORTH BRIDGE CREEK TRAIL
SODA LAKE
FENCE LINE
LOGGING ROAD LOOP
DAVY LAKE
SODA LK.
DAVY LAKE TRAIL
FOREST GROVE ROAD
SKI CABIN
BRIDGE CREEK
HAYFIELD LOOP
UPPER WILLOWDALE TRAIL
CAMEL LAKE
CAMEL LAKE TRAIL
N
UPPER WILLOWDALE CABIN
RED COACH
1 cm = 400 m (approx.)

RED COACH INN–COACH & WAGGON RECREATION NETWORK

Level of Difficulty: Beginner to Advanced
Base Elevation: 930 m
Length: 45-km network
Nearest Community: Trails begin at 100 Mile House
Camping or Accommodations: Red Coach Inn and 100 Mile House
Map: Trail map available from Red Coach Inn, 100 Mile House, B.C. V0K 2E0 or at Coach and Waggon Recreation Centre; trails are shown on Outdoor Recreation Council Map #1, 100 Mile House Region

DIRECTIONS

Trails begin across Highway 97 from Red Coach Inn and at the Coach and Waggon Recreation Centre at the north end of town.

DESCRIPTION

A series of cross-country trails varying in length from 3.2 km to 10 km have been laid out along Bridge Creek, north towards 103 Mile Lake and around 101 Mile Lake. They are maintained and groomed by the Red Coach Inn and Coach and Waggon Recreation Centre. The trails wind along Cariboo fences, through groves of trees and across open meadows, sometimes coming in sight of a cabin or lake. Trail status should be confirmed before use and a ski pass must be attached to your ski pole. Register at the Red Coach Inn or the Coach and Waggon Recreation Centre. At the Coach and Waggon there is a 4-km lighted track for night skiing as well as rentals, racquet courts and an exercise room.

108 RECREATIONAL RANCH NETWORK

Level of Difficulty: Beginner, Intermediate, Advanced
Length: 95 km of loops
Nearest Community: 100 Mile House, 10 km
Camping or Accommodations: 108 Motor Lodge
Map: Available from 108 Recreational Ranch

DIRECTIONS

Follow Highway 97 north 10 km from 100 Mile House.

DESCRIPTION

The 108 Recreational Ranch offers ski tourers a variety of challenges in an area of rolling hills, flat meadowland, frozen lakes and wooded countryside. The 95 km of trails groomed with a tracksetter are marked and laid out in loops suitable to various levels of skiers. There is a map at each intersection along the route. Ski trails at the 108 link up with many more kilometres of trails through the open country to the south, which in turn join up with the 100 Mile trail network.

Skiers are requested to indicate in the log book at the motor lodge desk the area to be skied in and the approximate time of return. Facilities at the 108 include a modern motor lodge with saunas, ski shop and rentals and a cross-country ski school. There are also outdoor skating

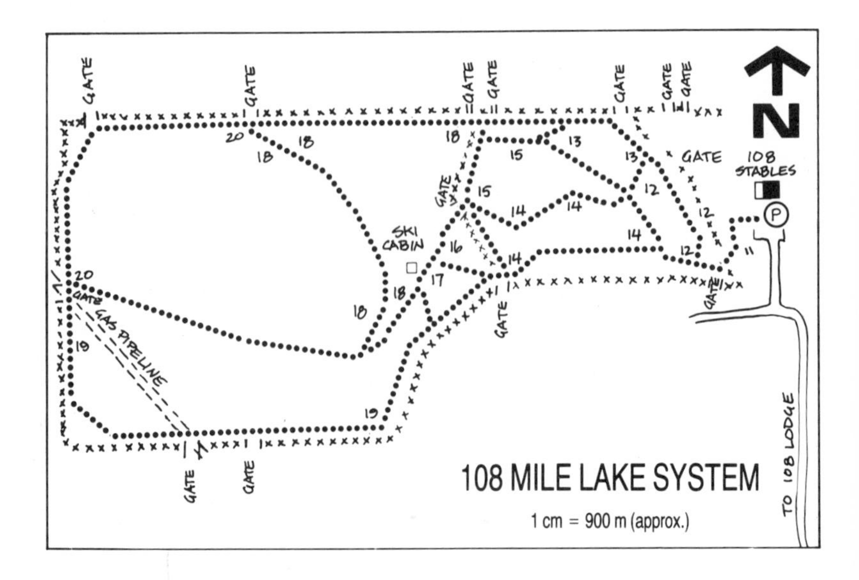

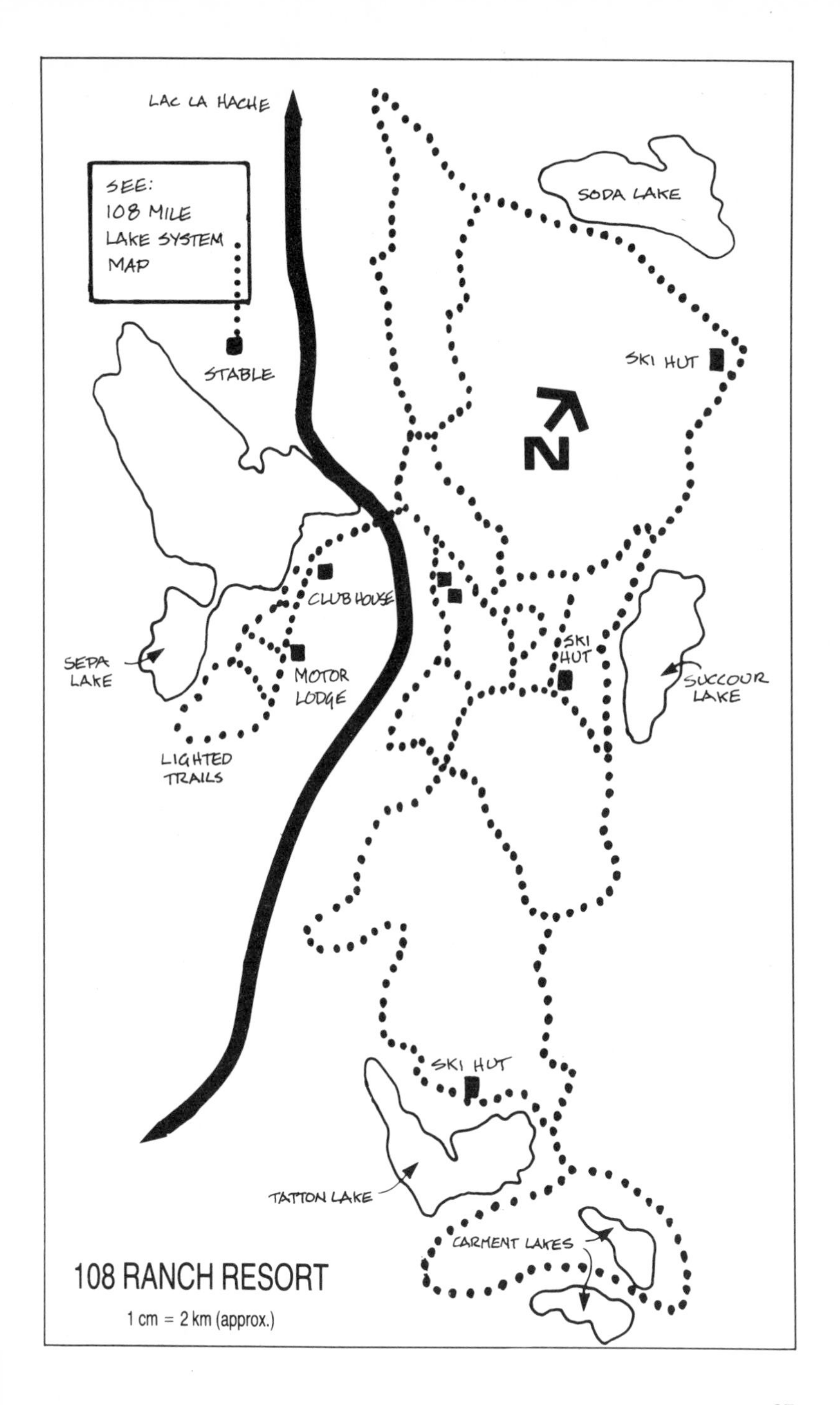
LAC LA HACHE
SEE:
108 MILE
LAKE SYSTEM
MAP
SODA LAKE
STABLE
SKI HUT
N
CLUB HOUSE
SEPA
LAKE
MOTOR
LODGE
SKI
HUT
SUCCOUR
LAKE
LIGHTED
TRAILS
SKI HUT
TATTON LAKE
CARMENT LAKES
108 RANCH RESORT
1 cm = 2 km (approx.)

and curling rinks, tobogganing, night skiing and skating, snowmobiling and ice fishing. For night skiing there is a 5-km lighted track around the golf course at the lodge.

SPRINGHOUSE TRAILS

Level of Difficulty: Beginner to Intermediate
Base Elevation: 914 m
Length: 60 km network
Nearest Community: Williams Lake, 19 km
Camping or Accommodations: Springhouse Trails Ranch and Williams Lake
Map: N.T.S. 1:50 000, 920/16 Springhouse

DIRECTIONS

Trails begin at or near Springhouse Trails Ranch, 19 km south of Williams Lake on Dog Creek Road.

DESCRIPTION

The ranch maintains a system of trails within its own fences—a series of loops around the lake and along fence lines. Depending on snow conditions and the guests' desires, the owners sometimes groom, or run a snowmobile over, other routes in the area, such as the Axe Lake Trail or the longer, more obscure route to Chimney Lake. The ranch has a simple trail map of these internal routes, although it is really not needed.

Chimney Lake is reached by following the power line south to an ill-defined left turn towards the lake. Check with the ranch to see if it has been located recently with a snowmobile. It is 36 km return, a long ski for one day.

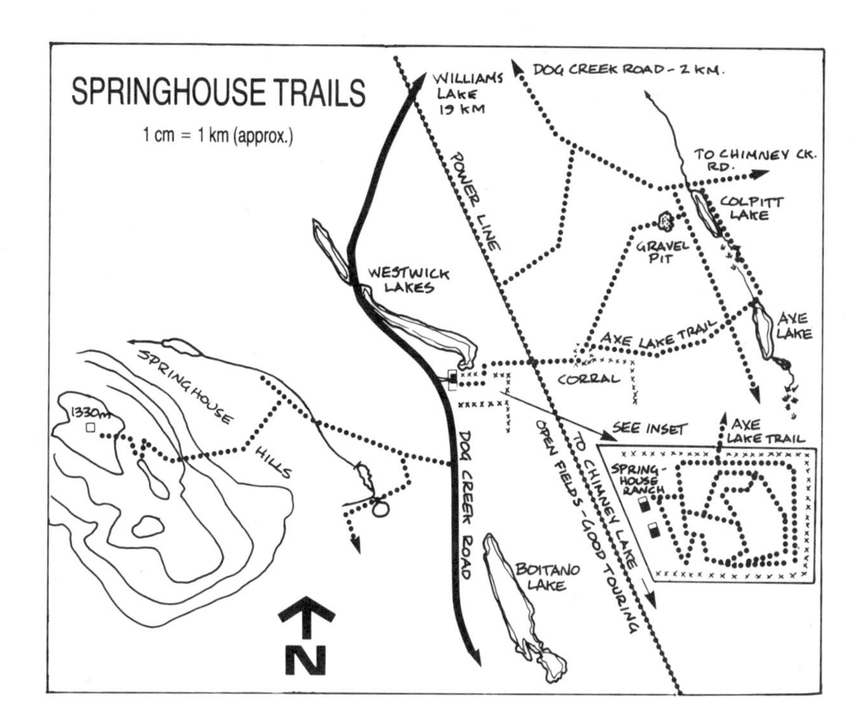

AXE LAKE TRAIL

Level of Difficulty: Intermediate
Base Elevation: 914 m
Return Length: 12 km, plus possible extensions
Vertical Drop: 60 m
Nearest Community: Williams Lake, 19 km
Camping or Accommodations: Springhouse Trails Ranch and Williams Lake
Map: N.T.S. 1:50 000, 920/16 Springhouse

DIRECTIONS

The trail begins at Springhouse Trails Ranch, although it can also be reached from the power line.

DESCRIPTION

From the ranch buildings the trail heads down a short slope to the end of Westwick Lake. It passes through a ranch fence and then climbs up a hill towards the power line. Cross the power line to a clearing and watch for a corral a few hundred metres farther on. Go around the corral and turn right. Do not continue on the road through the corral. Follow the fence line to the right and you will strike a lake trail which is easily followed from here.

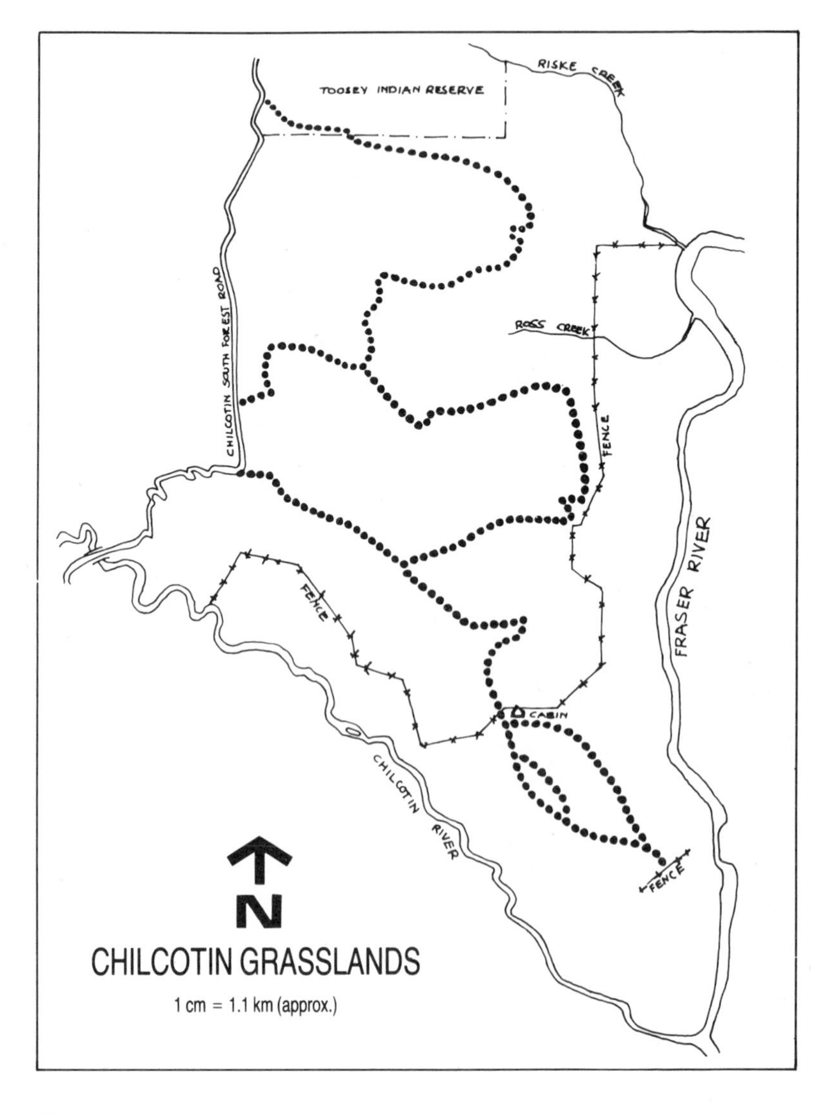

CHILCOTIN GRASSLANDS

1 cm = 1.1 km (approx.)

For a pleasant ski at the lake, head north along the shore of Colpitt Lake and, by a series of logging roads indicated on the accompanying map, make a loop back to the ranch.

CHILCOTIN GRASSLANDS

The rolling hills of the Chilcotin Grasslands west of Williams Lake are ideal for ski touring. You can wander in any direction you wish. South of Riske Creek, which is about 50 km west of Williams Lake on the Bella Coola highway, is a large area of benchland nestled between the Fraser and Chilcotin rivers. This is the home of a herd of California bighorn sheep and if you ski here you will have a good chance of seeing these magnificent mammals. It is important not to harass them, as they require all their energy to survive in the winter months.

The accompanying map indicates the summer roads through the area. They will not necessarily be evident after a good snowfall, but are a guideline to what is accessible. The roads are marked with signs about 0.3 m high. Generally the precipitation is quite low in this desertlike area, so the snowfall is not usually very heavy.

HANCEVILLE AREA

In the Hanceville area, which is about 94 km west of Williams Lake, accommodations and ski touring are available through the TH Guest Ranch. There are several packed trails in snow which ranges from 0.5 m to 1 m deep. During the short ski season, usually from December 15 to the end of January, miles of virgin snow can be found on the benches along the Chilcotin River and on logging roads in the area.

As well as rustic log cabins, the ranch has a main lodge. Other activities offered include sleigh riding, moonlight ski tours and square dancing.

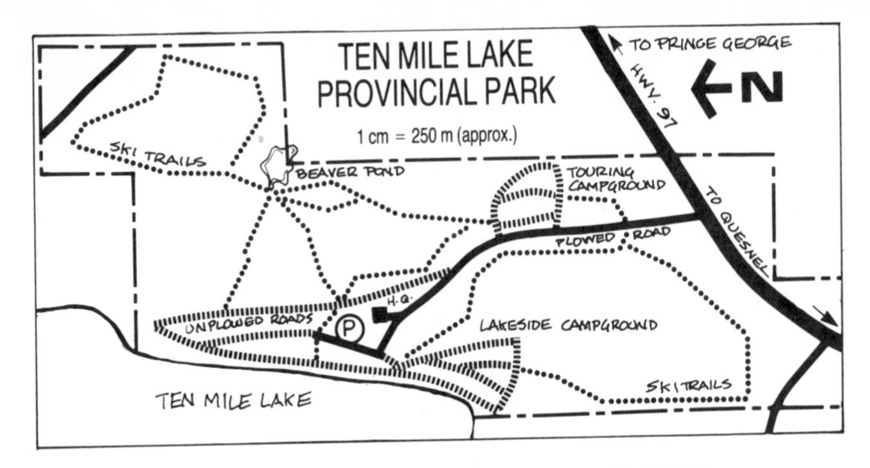

TEN MILE LAKE PROVINCIAL PARK

Level of Difficulty: Beginner
Base Elevation: 707 m
Length: 10-km network
Nearest Community: Quesnel, 11 km
Camping or Accommodations: Camping at park; Quesnel
Map: Trail map available from Ministry of Lands, Parks and Housing, Parks and Outdoor Recreation Division, Barkerville, B.C. V0K 1B0

DIRECTIONS

The park is located 11 km north of Quesnel on Highway 97.

DESCRIPTION

This small park, 240 ha, has 10 km of looped trails for cross-country use. The trails loop around the beaver pond, along Ten Mile Lake and through the campground roads.

WELLS-BARKERVILLE AREA

There are several good backcountry and cross-country tours in this area, the most obvious being the Bowron Lake tour, suitable for those who want a long but flat ski. Another long tour goes over the hump of Yanks

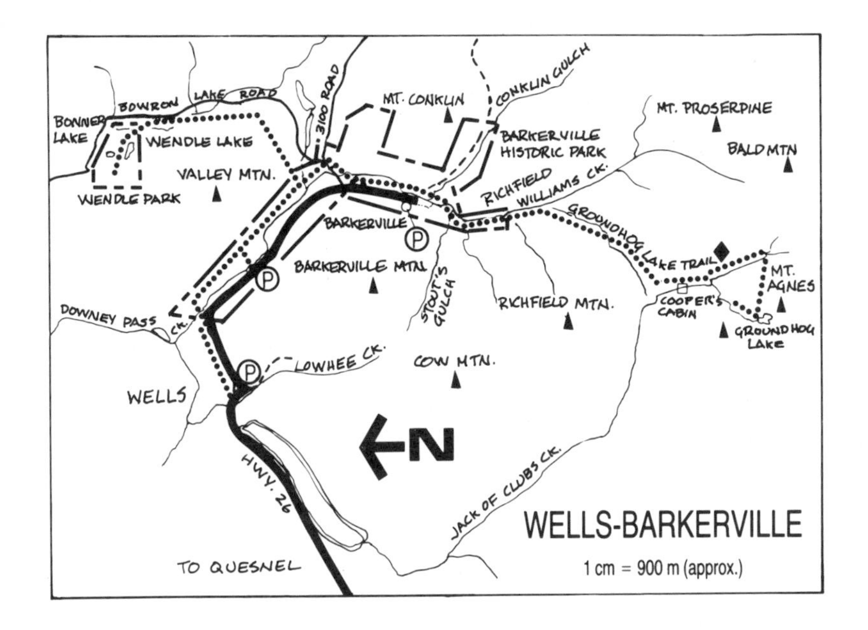

Peak to Keithly Creek. Most cross-country skiers, though, will be interested in those that use the valley bottom, such as the trails to Wendle Lake and along Williams Creek, as shown on the accompanying map. Another popular route is through the old town to Richfield, and then on towards Groundhog Lake.

GROUNDHOG LAKE TRAIL

Level of Difficulty: Intermediate to Advanced
Base Elevation: 900 m
Return Length: 16 km
Vertical Drop: 500 m
Nearest Community: Wells, 5 km
Camping or Accommodations: Wells and Quesnel
Map: Trail map available from Ministry of Lands, Parks and Housing, Parks and Outdoor Recreation Division, Barkerville, B.C. V0K 1B0

DIRECTIONS

Trail begins at the parking lot in Barkerville.

DESCRIPTION

This tour takes approximately four hours and is suitable only for experienced skiers. All skiers should carry emergency gear. Fluorescent orange markers flag the trail, which is kept up by the Ministry of Lands, Parks and Housing, the Ministry of Forests and Cariboo Ski Touring Club.

The trail goes through Barkerville to Richfield, then up an arm of Williams Creek, over to Jack of Clubs Creek and on to Groundhog Lake.

BOWRON LAKE PROVINCIAL PARK CIRCUIT

Level of Difficulty: Advanced; winter camping and survival skills are necessary
Base Elevation: 896 m
Return Length: 116-km loop
Vertical Drop: 52 m
Nearest Communities: Wells, 28 km; Quesnel, 112 km
Camping or Accommodations: Lodges closed in winter; some shelters on circuit but skiers must have complete equipment for winter camping; accommodations in Wells
Map: Park brochure and map available from Ministry of Lands, Parks and Housing, Outdoor Recreation Division; waterproof map from Ministry of Environment, Survey and Resource Mapping Branch

DIRECTIONS

Follow Highway 26 east from Quesnel and then take the north fork beyond Wells. The road from Wells to Bowron Lake is plowed in winter but chains should be carried.

DESCRIPTION

The unique aspect of Bowron Lake Provincial Park is its system of six major lakes and connecting waterways that provide a natural circuit ideal for canoeists and, more recently, ski tourers. Travel on the lakes is usually fairly easy and can be done from January to mid-March, with February and early March being the best times. Snow and ice conditions vary greatly and change quickly. The average snow depth in the park is

0.5 m to 1.2 m, and though the amount of snow on the ice-covered lake fluctuates, it is usually wind-packed.

The Parks Branch has some advice on the route: "It is suggested to travel the circuit counter-clockwise starting with Bowron Lake. Break up is earlier on the west side. The three portage trails between Isaac Lake and Park Headquarters are usually packed and easy to travel."

Lake inlets and outlets and all moving water must be carefully checked for weak ice and snow-covered water. Information must be obtained from local park staff immediately before any tour.

Other recommendations of the Parks Branch regarding safety include:

— Register with Park Headquarters prior to your departure to obtain the latest news and conditions.
— Three people should be the minimum party size; four people is ideal.
— Travel several feet apart, and stay on or close to shore wherever possible.

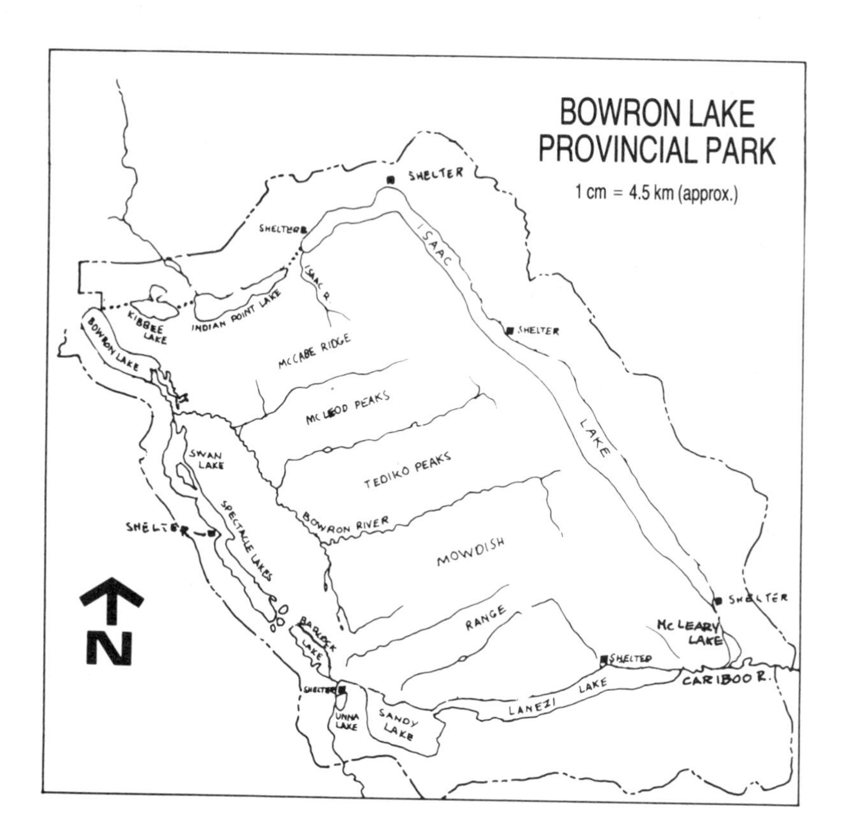

— Be especially careful on the rivers; the thickness of ice can change rapidly.
— Make a wide circle where streams enter the lakes.
— Watch for wet spots, depressions and different-coloured snow.
— Underground springs are active even at subzero temperatures.
— Wide cracks are known to appear on some of the lakes.
— Be extremely watchful after a fresh snowfall danger spots may be hidden.
— Do not camp or stop on avalanche chutes along Isaac and Lanezi lakes. They are easily recognized as treeless fingers reaching from the lakes to the mountaintops.
— Complete equipment for winter camping is required. Do not rely on reaching a shelter every night.

Wildlife that may be seen in the park includes moose, wolves, fishers, otters and owls.

Raven tracks in snow

THOMPSON-OKANAGAN REGION

The hills and valleys that form the Thompson-Okanagan provide some of the best contours in British Columbia for ski touring. Though the valley often appears clouded over, most of the ski areas are high enough on the surrounding hills to be often bathed in sun above the clouds, unaffected by the temperature inversion. Do not be misled by cloudy conditions in the valley; check out the weather further to find out what the conditions are on the upper slopes.

The area generally is one of only moderate precipitation, so that the skiing season of the lower areas varies considerably from year to year. On the mountains, the skiing season is usually from December to the end of April.

SNOWPATCH SKI AREA

Level of Difficulty: Beginner to Intermediate
Base Elevation: 1300 m
Return Length: 8 km
Vertical Drop: 115 m
Nearest Community: Princeton, 8 km
Camping or Accommodations: Motels in Princeton

DIRECTIONS

Beginning on Highway 3 at Princeton, signs indicate the route to follow to Snowpatch, first heading north through the town of Princeton, along the Coalmont Road, and then branching right to the ski area.

DESCRIPTION

Snowpatch is an excellent Beginner area with trails meandering up and down gentle slopes in some open country, but mostly through pine and fir forests. For those who are looking for more of a challenge, some of the easier downhill routes provide an Intermediate cross-country experience. It is a fine area to observe the tracks of wildlife. At times the hills are riddled with deer tracks, and it is interesting to note where they browse and where they sink into the deep snow. Often their tracks can be seen following along the cross-country trails, where the going is a little easier. There are many rabbit imprints crossing the routes and occasional tracks of squirrels, chipmunks, weasels, coyotes and elk. And of course as long as the tracks are around there is always the chance of seeing the animals that make them. Black-capped chickadees can be seen and heard amongst the trees, and there is lots of lichen around.

On clear days there are scenic views of the Similkameen Valley, as well as mountain vistas all the way to Penticton.

The cross-country trails begin just west of the downhill ski area. There are no maps and only occasional markers, but it is easy to follow the trails which loop around, some going above the downhill ski area.

The day lodge by the parking area has a snack bar and a few cross-country rentals. Minor repairs can be done there as well.

MOUNT BALDY SKI AREA

Level of Difficulty: Intermediate
Base Elevation: 1880 m
Return Length: 8 km
Vertical Drop: 140 m
Nearest Community: Bridesville, 18 km
Camping or Accommodations: Motels in Osoyoos

DIRECTIONS

Go 37 km east from Osoyoos on Highway 3 and then take a left turn at Rock Creek Canyon Bridge; go the remaining 17 km to the Baldy day lodge, keeping left at the junction about 9 km along the road.

DESCRIPTION

A flagged cross-country trail which has been cut by the Forest Service starts just below the ski lodge and climbs up a knoll that can be seen from the road. The route circles the knoll, meandering across the alternately treed and open slope, and returns through the downhill area. There are many panoramic views along the way. If you want to skip most of the climbing, you can take the lift up the mountain to ski and get a fine view looking north in the direction of Naramata.

There is a coffee bar and a licensed lounge in the day lodge at Baldy, and space for camper or trailer camping. For weather reports, phone Radio Operator Grand Forks and ask for Baldy Ski Area.

CARMI X-COUNTRY SKI TRAILS

Level of Difficulty: Beginner to Advanced
Base Elevation: 970 m
Return Length: Up to 8 km
Vertical Drop: 550 m
Nearest Community: Penticton, 3.5 km
Camping or Accommodations: Penticton

DIRECTIONS

Go east from Penticton on Carmi Road; the trail heads are along this road between 3.5 km and 8 km from Penticton.

DESCRIPTION

A Canada Works Grant in 1978 first enabled the Penticton Outdoor Club to clear old logging roads so they could be used for cross-country skiing. The marked trails all head uphill on the north side of the Carmi Road. Grades are generally moderate, but there are some steep sections.

APEX ALPINE SKI AREA

Apex Alpine is situated midway between the Pacific Coast and the Rocky Mountains. Though there are no mapped or groomed cross-country trails at this downhill ski complex, much of the country is perfect for ski touring. The downhill ski complex from which all the ski trails start is located in Apex Mountain Provincial Park. A couple of the routes listed below are on the mountain within the park and provide panoramic views of snow-blanketed Okanagan hills; another leads out of the park to Nickel Plate Lake in Nickel Lake Provincial Park; the last is a more lengthy excursion requiring more preparation and transportation arrangements. The alpine meadow between Apex and Beaconsfield is also a good area for touring.

Facilities at Apex include lifts, a day lodge, cafeteria, restaurant, grocery store, hot tubs, lounge and accommodations. There is a full-time ski patrol. Dry snow conditions prevail from the end of November to the end of March. Apex Alpine snow reports are available at Penticton: telephone (604) 493-3606 (24-hour recorded reports).

Base Elevation: 1830 m
Nearest Community: Penticton, 35 km
Camping or Accommodations: Accommodations and overnight R.V. hookups at Apex Alpine; Penticton

DIRECTIONS

Follow the Green Mountain Road west from Penticton. After 24 km take the right fork, which leads to the parking lots; skiers from the coast can take a shortcut by making a left turn off Highway 3 approximately 6 km north of Olalla and going north to the junction with Green Mountain Road.

MOUNT RIORDAN TRAIL

Level of Difficulty: Intermediate
Return Length: Approximately 6 km
Vertical Drop: 275 m

The trail to follow from the lodge begins halfway down the hill behind the bunny tow. This trail winds through wooded terrain around the back of the hill. Junctions lead south to Beaconsfield Mountain and east to Nickel Plate Lake and Hedley. Keep right at these junctions to follow

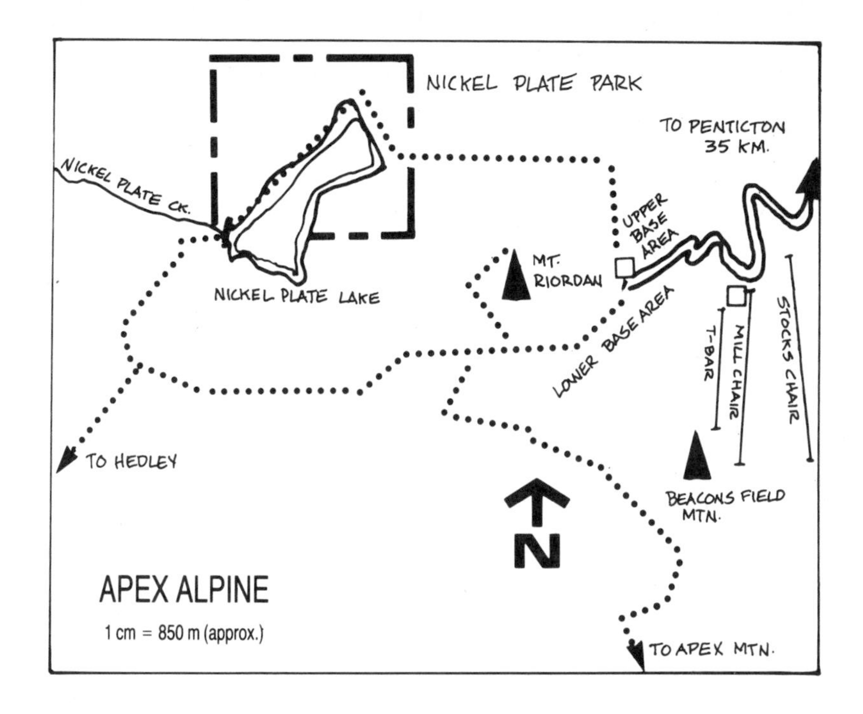

the old logging road which goes north, ascending the hill from the back side. The uphill portion of this route provides great views of the surrounding countryside, and makes for a very quick but enjoyable return descent, retracing tracks to the trail head.

BEACONSFIELD MOUNTAIN TRAIL

Level of Difficulty: Intermediate
Return Length: Approximately 10 km
Vertical Drop: 350 m

The trail up Beaconsfield is similar to the Mount Riordan Trail: in each case old logging roads are followed around and up the back of the mountains. The Beaconsfield trail begins behind the bunny tow and follows the same route as for Riordan until it branches south and then gradually up. Once you are on the mountain the hills are fairly open and can be skied as desired. The simplest way back is just to retrace the route.

NICKEL PLATE LAKE TRAIL

Level of Difficulty: Intermediate
Length: Approximately 12 km
Vertical Drop: 100 m

Nickel Plate Lake can be reached by beginning as for the previous two trails, following the trail behind the bunny tow and continuing east past the junctions that go left and right, and following the right fork of the T-junction. An alternative approach is to drive beyond the private houses on the road to the upper lodge area, and turn right onto the Nickel Plate forestry road. Park and ski up the switchback road.

The initial uphill grade is followed by gentle rolling terrain through lodgepole pine and spruce to Nickel Plate Lake. A steep downhill portion near the lake should be taken with care. Proceed west along the north shore of the lake to a coffer dam. Head south until a junction is reached and then east (left) and return to Apex Alpine ski area by the trail behind the bunny tow. The north end of Nickel Plate Lake is located within Nickel Plate Provincial Park. The only grades to watch are the switchbacks at the beginning of the loop, an area by the lake, and the logging road at the end of the route.

APEX-HEDLEY TRAIL

Level of Difficulty: Intermediate
Length: Approximately 22 km
Vertical Drop: 1400 m

Though the skiing of this route is not difficult in itself, those attempting it should be experienced skiers who are competent with map and compass and well-equipped for the tour. The route follows old logging and mining roads but is unmarked; without topographical maps and compass it is possible to wander onto the wrong side road. The other consideration is the arranging of transportation to both ends of the route, which are about 60 km apart by road.

The joy of this trail is that you descend 1400 m more than you climb. The route begins behind the bunny tow at Apex Alpine. It follows the trail described in the Mount Riordan Trail, passes the junction to Riordan, the turnoff to Beaconsfield, and turns left where Nickel Plate Lake Trail forks right. It traverses woodland and subalpine, and follows an old logging road and power line. Though the entire route could be described as scenic, the views become breathtaking where the trail overlooks the snaking Similkameen River, parallelled by the Hope-Princeton highway. The final section of the route zigzags steeply down to the

Similkameen Valley, meeting Highway 3 about 2.5 km east of Hedley.

A point of interest on this ski route is the Nickel Plate Mine located on Nickel Plate Mountain high above the town of Hedley. Discovered in the 1890s, the mine was in almost continuous production from 1904 until 1955, yielding ore rich in gold, silver, copper and arsenic. Some of the dilapidated mine buildings can still be seen on the mountain. The scar of the tramway which transported ore to the mill is evident above the town. It is claimed that over $45 million in gold was taken from Nickel Plate Mountain.

CHUTE LAKE

Level of Difficulty: Intermediate
Base Elevation: 1186 m at Chute Lake
Return Length: Up to 16 km
Vertical Drop: 450 m
Nearest Community: Naramata, 19 km
Camping or Accommodations: Penticton

DIRECTIONS

From Penticton follow the Naramata road 13 km to the Naramata—Chute Lake junction; then keep right for 7 km and take another right turn. The road from here is a fairly steady climb, zigzagging up through pine and fir forest another 10 km to a view ahead of Chute Lake. This final section of road may be quite icy, but there is a good pull-off or turnaround point about 4 km along it.

DESCRIPTION

Chute Lake, at an elevation of 1200 m, is just high enough in the Okanagan hills to have good snow for ski touring when lower levels are lacking. Another advantage of this elevation is that Chute Lake may be basking in sunshine when the sky is low and overcast at Penticton.

From the point at which Chute Lake can be viewed (0.2 km before Chute Lake Resort is reached), a ski trail follows an old road down to the right, across the railroad bed and then gradually uphill, winding through lodgepole pine/spruce-fir forest. Eventually Elinor Lake, a water supply reservoir, is reached, and farther along the trail is Naramata Lake. An alternative route is to fork left at Elinor Lake and continue uphill to Big Meadow Lake.

Watch for animal tracks in the snow—there are lots of snowshoe hares in the area—and coyotes may be heard. Deer tracks may be either mule deer or whitetail. Bird sightings include white-winged crossbill, spruce grouse and mountain chickadee.

The trail south from Chute Lake is only one of several routes that can be taken from this area. For example, the railway tracks can be used as a trail and followed either north towards Kelowna or south to Naramata. Another trail leaves the Chute Lake road several kilometres before Chute Lake and climbs south to a microwave tower.

PEACHLAND TRAIL BLAZERS SKI AREA

Level of Difficulty: Beginner to Advanced
Base Elevation: 1000 m
Length: 30-km network
Vertical Drop: 500 m
Nearest Community: Peachland, 12 km
Camping or Accommodations: Motels in Peachland

DIRECTIONS

Follow the Brenda Mines Road about 12 km west from Peachland. There is a parking area on the northwest side of the road.

DESCRIPTION

A trail network of over 30 km runs parallel to the Brenda Mines Road and follows the nearby power line cut. There are fifteen numbered trails marked according to difficulty and maintained by the Peachland Trailblazers Club. There is also a cabin, an outhouse and a shelter.

HEADWATERS LAKE SKI AREA

Level of Difficulty: Beginner to Intermediate
Base Elevation: 1300 m
Return Length: 11 km
Vertical Drop: Minimal
Nearest Community: Peachland, 26 km
Camping or Accommodations: Winterized cabins at Headwaters Fishing Camp; motels in Peachland

DIRECTIONS

From Peachland go west on the Brenda Mines Road about 12 km to a junction. Take the left fork another 14 km to Headwaters Lake.

DESCRIPTION

Headwaters Fishing Camp is located on a beautiful lake in a mountain forest. It offers three groomed trails around the lodge and lake for cross-country skiing. Other winter activities include ice fishing, outdoor ice skating and snowmobiling.

Headwaters Lake Trail, red, 4-km loop around the lake.
June Lake Trail, green, 6-km loop including June Lake; 4 km are part of the Headwaters Lake Trail.
Camp Trail, yellow, 1-km loop near lodge.

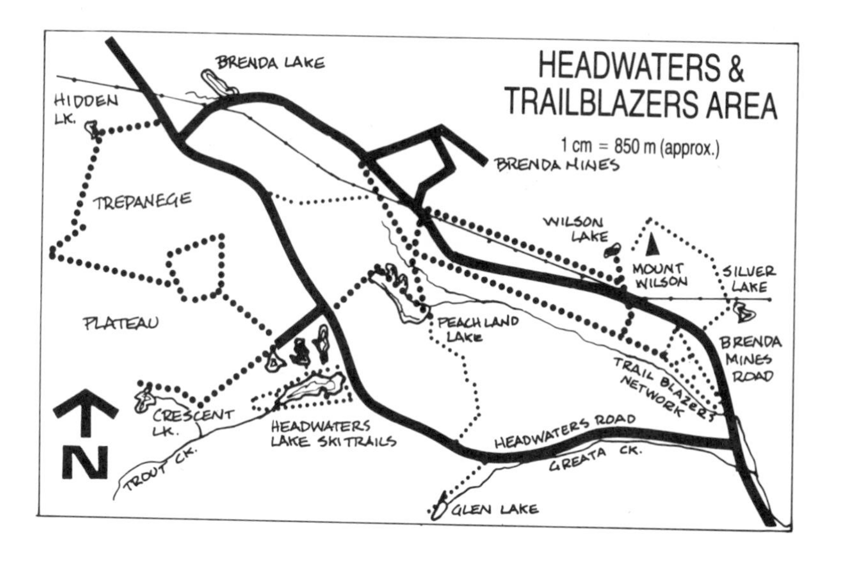

TELEMARK X-COUNTRY SKI AREA

Level of Difficulty: Beginner to Advanced
Base Elevation: 1150 m
Return Length: 1.5 km to 10 km
Vertical Drop: 270 m
Nearest Community: Westbank, 11 km
Camping or Accommodations: Westbank and Kelowna

DIRECTIONS

Go 1 km south from Westbank on Highway 97, then follow Last Mountain Road for 10 km. There is a parking area just west of the road.

DESCRIPTION

A total of 45 km of Forest Service trails have been marked, mapped and groomed, with plans for expansion. Green, blue and red designations indicate the difficulty of the trails. The Telemark Ski Club grooms this network using a double-track snowmobile and track setter. In addition to maintaining this trail system in fine condition, the club also sponsors racing and has developed a biathlon circuit.

BEAR LAKE MAIN ROAD

Level of Difficulty: Beginner to Intermediate
Base Elevation: 670 m
Return Length: More than 30 km
Vertical Drop: 1260 m
Nearest Community: Kelowna, 11 km
Camping or Accommodations: Kelowna

DIRECTIONS

Go north from Westbank and leave Highway 97 at Westside Road; follow it north for 10 km. Then head west on Bear Lake Main Road another 7 km.

DESCRIPTION
A logging road network northwest of Westbank offers fine opportunities for ski touring on weekends on the plateau country above Okanagan Lake. Weekdays should be avoided, or at the very least, extreme caution should be used as logging trucks frequent the Bear Lake Main Road.

BIG WHITE SKI AREA

Base Elevation: 1800 m
Nearest Community: Kelowna, 58 km
Camping or Accommodations: Camping on mountain—register with Information Centre in Village Lodge; motel and lodge accommodations at Ski Village and in Kelowna

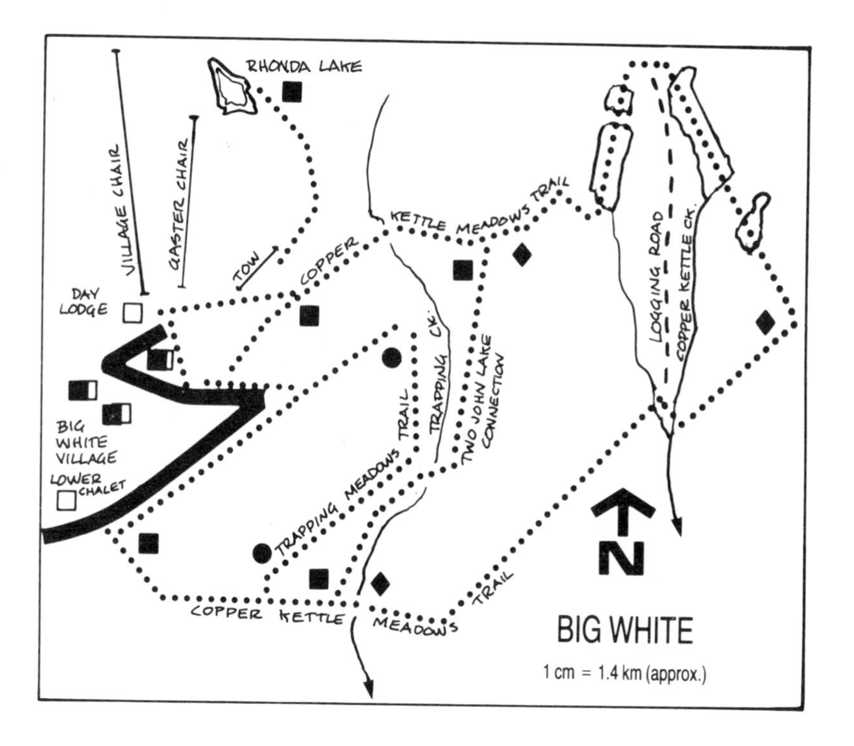

DIRECTIONS

Follow Highway 33 east from Kelowna for 35 km; take a left turn and continue another 22 km to Big White Ski Village.

Winter travellers on Highway 33 should carry chains or use good tread winter tires.

DESCRIPTION

Located 1800 m up in the mountains east of Kelowna, the Big White Ski Village, an alpine resort community, claims to be the highest ski area in British Columbia. It is well known for its powder snow, and for having snow longer than most other areas. The ski season in a normal year runs from about 15 November to 15 April. In 1978, 25 km of cross-country trails were established, and are kept marked and groomed. They pass through the mountainous terrain surrounding the ski village.

A large number of mammals have been seen on the slopes of Big White. Watch for signs of whitetail and mule deer, moose, coyotes, wolverines, cougars, marmots, martins, rabbits, weasels, fishers, squirrels, chipmunks and porcupines.

Cross-country ski rentals are available on the mountain for adults and children 10 years of age and older. Lessons are also available from the Brian James Ski School.

Besides being able to accommodate over 1000 skiers, facilities at Big White Ski Village include a day lodge, cafeteria, dining room, grocet-eria, electrical hookups for campers, propane filling station, showers, laundromat and day care. Babysitting is free during weekdays. There is free alpine skiing at night, as well as many social activities.

TRAPPING MEADOWS TRAIL

Level of Difficulty: Beginner
Return Length: 5 km
Vertical Drop: 76 m

The easiest of the three routes at Big White, this trail begins at the Lower Chalet and circles around to the left through wooded areas and across several natural meadows. Like all the cross-country trails on the mountain, there are route signs at all junctions. This is Route #1 and is marked by green circles. Map boards are located at the Lower Chalet and Village Lodge (day lodge). Distances along the trail are marked at 0.5-km intervals.

TWO JOHN LAKE CONNECTION

Level of Difficulty: Intermediate
Return Length: 8 km
Vertical Drop: 150 m

Route #2 at Big White is marked with a blue diamond. This trail begins at the Lower Chalet and follows the same path as Route #1 for about 1 km. It branches left a short distance after #1 branches off, then loops around a larger circle and rejoins #1 for the last portion.

COPPER KETTLE MEADOWS TRAIL

Level of Difficulty: Advanced
Return Length: 12.5 km
Vertical Drop: 180 m

Route #3, marked with red triangles, is the most difficult of the three routes listed here. It begins with the other trails at the Lower Chalet, separates from them to loop higher up the mountain through some logged-off areas and across several natural meadows, then picks up the other trails as it descends back to the starting point.

McCULLOCH SKI AREA NETWORK

Level of Difficulty: Beginner to Advanced
Base Elevation: 1280 m
Return Length: 3.5 km to 25 km; approximately 90 km total
Nearest Community: Kelowna, 38 km
Camping or Accommodations: Cabins at McCulloch; Kelowna

DIRECTIONS

Follow Highway 33 east from Kelowna 38 km to a parking lot for the Nordic cross-country trails and Joe Rich Summit; go about 3 km farther down Highway 33 and turn right onto McCulloch Road, continuing another 4 km to another parking lot for the McCulloch ski trails and a map of all the trails.

A sign near the beginning of Highway 33 reminds motorists to carry chains or use good tread winter tires.

DESCRIPTION

McCulloch is a railway stop on the Canadian Pacific Railway's Kettle Valley line which passes through the area on its circuitous route between the Okanagan and Kettle valleys; it is located on the north side of Hydraulic Creek reservoir, one of the McCulloch lakes. There are two networks of cross-country trails centred around McCulloch. One of these has been developed and maintained by White Mountain Fish Camp in co-operation with McClure Sports World in Kelowna. The use of fishing resorts for cross-country skiing is becoming a popular way to extend use of facilities into the winter months. The second trail system, referred to as the Nordic Trails, is a joint effort between the Nordic Ski Club and the Ministry of Forests. Each network has trails for all levels of skiers. The rolling hills around and over which the ski tracks pass make this a very good area for learning to ski. The trails meander through pine forests and meadows. A log cabin on one of the routes provides a good lunch stop. Occasionally are seen tracks of some of the small mammals in the area, such as rabbits, coyotes, porcupines and skunks.

There is a map of the trail systems by the White Mountain Fish Camp parking lot, and all the trails are well marked. Ski rentals are available. Following is a list of the trails in the area:

McCULLOCH TRAILS

	Length Return
Beginner	
Blue	6.0 km
Yellow	3.5 km
Intermediate	
Red	12.5 km
Advanced	
Red Extension	25.0 km

NORDIC TRAILS

Beginner	
Blue	5.0 km
Intermediate	
Orange	11.0 km
Red	12.0 km
Advanced	
Red Extension	16.0 km

The Advanced Red Extension trails listed above overlap.

POSTILL–BEAVER LAKE SKI TRAILS

Level of Difficulty: Beginner to Intermediate
Base Elevation: 1500 m
Length: 65-km network
Vertical Drop: 150 m
Nearest Communities: Kelowna, 19 km; Winfield, 16 km
Camping or Accommodations: Kelowna and Winfield

DIRECTIONS

From Highway 97, turn east at the north end of Kelowna airport. Follow signs for 19 km to Postill Lake. A second access point is from Winfield on Highway 97: turn east on Beaver Lake Road and travel 16 km to Beaver Lake.

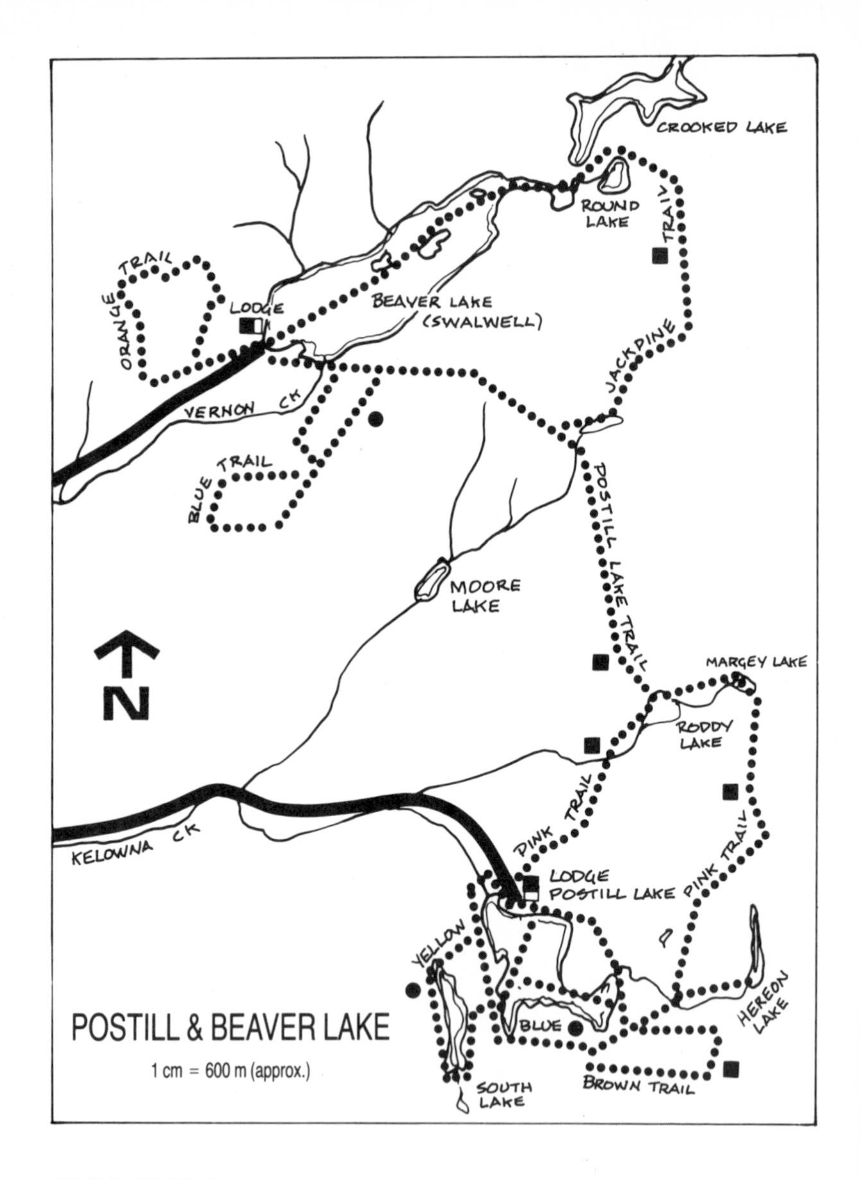

DESCRIPTION

Trails in the vicinity of Beaver Lake (Swalwell Lake on some maps) join with those in the Postill Lake area to form a loose network of about 65 km of trails. Since there are two access roads, it would be a pleasant route to do as a round trip, leaving one vehicle at each end. The trail network around Beaver Lake is sometimes known as the Grizzly Hills Trails.

GRIZZLY HILLS TRAILS

Orange Trail, Intermediate, 5-km loop.
Blue Trail, Beginner, 8-km loop.
Jackpine Trail, Intermediate, 16 km along Beaver Lake with a loop past Round Lake back to Beaver Lake Lodge.
Postill Lake Trail, Intermediate, 11-km trail south to Postill Lake.

POSTILL LAKE TRAILS

Blue Trail, Beginner, 7.5-km loop around Postill Lake.
Green Trail, Beginner, 4.4-km loop to east of Postill Lake.
Yellow Trail, Beginner, 6.8-km loop around South Lake.
Pink Trail, Intermediate, 10.8-km loop to Margey Lake with a return through Karen Meadows to lodge.
Brown Trail, Intermediate, 11-km loop to east of Postill Lake.

SILVER STAR SKI AREA

Level of Difficulty: Beginner to Intermediate
Base Elevation: 1402 m
Return Length: 20 km total
Vertical Drop: 240 m
Nearest Community: Vernon, 22 km
Camping or Accommodations: Vernon

DIRECTIONS

Head north on Highway 97 from Vernon and turn east onto Silver Star Road at Village Green Inn. Turn left onto Repeater Station Road just before the downhill area. Drive 2 km to parking lot on left fork.

DESCRIPTION

Nordic skiers were using Silver Star long before downhill skiers. The North Okanagan Ski Club has developed a network of trails on the subalpine meadows northwest of the downhill complex. The marked and groomed routes start from the cross-country ski parking lot which is 2 km from Silver Star Road.

- Sovereign Lake Trail, Beginner, 1.6-km loop.
- Woodland Bell Trail, Intermediate, 4.8-km loop.
- Mystery Trail, Intermediate, 5.5-km loop.
- Black Prince Trail, Intermediate, 3.6-km loop from its junction with Mystery.

STUSSI'S CROSS-COUNTRY CENTRE

Nearest Community: Falkland, 14 km
Camping or Accommodations: Lodge at Stussi's Cross-Country Centre; Vernon
Map: Available from Stussi Sports in Vernon

DIRECTIONS

From Vernon take Highway 97 north for 35 km; take a left turn onto Cedar Hill Road and continue along it for approximately 3 km until you reach the lodge.

DESCRIPTION

Located in the hills south of Falkland, Stussi's Cross-Country Centre is a resort catering to cross-country skiers, with a lodge, ski rentals, a ski

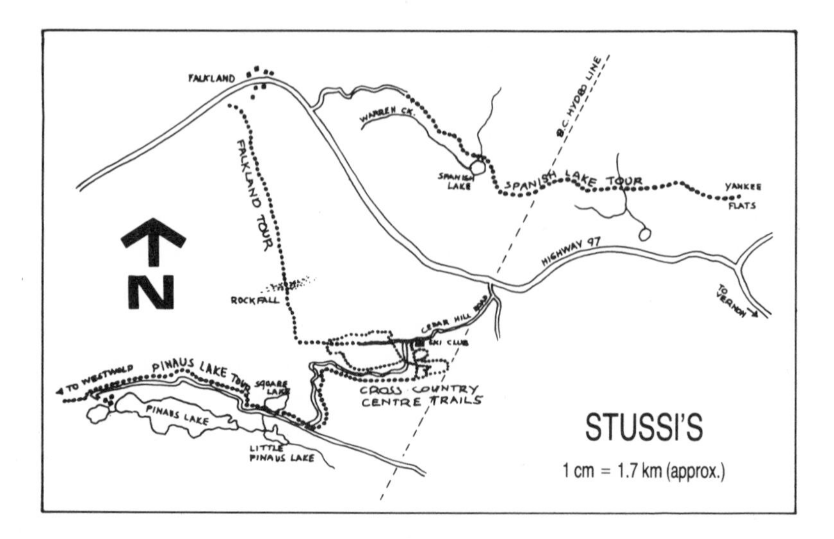

school and approximately 60 km of trails. The rustic lodge has 22 bunk beds, two washrooms, a big kitchen and a dining area. Special rates are offered for children ages 8 to 12 for lessons and rentals. There is a trail fee except for children under 8. Snowshoeing, tobogganing, innertubing and night skiing are also available. Watch for signs of deer, rabbits and squirrels while on the trails.

CROSS-COUNTRY CENTRE TRAILS

Level of Difficulty: Beginner to Advanced
Length: Up to 5 km

A system of trails for all levels of skiers fans out in three directions from the centre. They are all located within about 1 km of Cedar Hill Road.

PINAUS LAKE TOUR

Level of Difficulty: Advanced
Length: 16 km one way
Vertical Drop: 365 m

This trail follows an old road which winds 8 km up to Square Lake, and then continues another 8 km to the far end of Pinaus Lake. The return trip can be made by retracing the route back to the Cross-Country Centre or by arranging a pick-up ahead on the road which heads to Pinaus Lake from a point on Highway 97 about 3 km east of Westwold.

FALKLAND TOUR

Level of Difficulty: Advanced
Length: 13 km one way
Vertical Drop: 120 m

This route heads west and then north to the small community of Falkland. There is one area of rockfall to watch out for about 2 km along the trail. This is another route for which it is advantageous to arrange transportation to both ends for a one-way ski tour.

SPANISH LAKE TOUR

Level of Difficulty: Advanced
Return Length: 26 km
Vertical Drop: 150 m

To reach the starting point for this ski tour, take the side road east of Falkland to Warren Creek and drive along it about 3 km to where the road approaches the creek. The ski trail climbs from this point to Spanish Lake and then continues across a hydro right-of-way and east another 7 km to an area called Yankee Flats. Return is back along the same trail.

WHITE LAKE SKI TRAILS

Level of Difficulty: Beginner to Advanced
Length: 40 km total
Nearest Community: Salmon Arm, 25 km
Camping or Accommodations: Motels in Salmon Arm; Shady Shore Camping
Map: Trail map available from Shady Shore Camping, R.R. #1, Sorrento, B.C. V0E 2W0

DIRECTIONS

White Lake lies east of the Trans-Canada Highway between Chase and Salmon Arm. It is reached by a road from Balmoral if travelling east and an alternative route closer to Tappen if travelling west.

DESCRIPTION

This year-round facility has a total of 40 km of trails across the lake and to the east. In winter, all the trails are double track-set. A log cabin is available for warmups and snacks. The owners cater to families and clubs and also offer ice skating, horse-drawn sleigh rides, horse-skiing, tobogganing and ice fishing. We suggest obtaining a trail map before starting out.

SKIMIKEN SKI TRAILS

Level of Difficulty: Beginner to Intermediate
Return Length: 16 km total
Nearest Community: Salmon Arm, 13 km
Camping or Accommodations: Motels in Salmon Arm
Map: Trail map available from Salmon Arm Chamber of Commerce, P.O. Box 999, Salmon Arm, B.C. V0E 2T0

DIRECTIONS

Take the Trans-Canada Highway northwest of Salmon Arm 13 km to the Tappen overpass. Turn left and follow the paved road past Skimiken Nursery. Watch for signs.

DESCRIPTION

A number of short trails, planned by the Shuswap Outdoors Club, are popular with local skiers. An annual 10-km ski race is held here.

LARCH HILLS NETWORK

Level of Difficulty: Beginner to Advanced
Base Elevation: 1100 m
Length: 150-km network
Vertical Drop: 1500 m
Nearest Community: Salmon Arm, 20 km
Camping or Accommodations: Motels in Salmon Arm
Map: A detailed map of the trail system has been published by Shuswap Outdoors Club and is available by mail for $5.50 from Shuswap Outdoors, P.O. Box 485, Salmon Arm, B.C. V0E 2T0, or from local stores.

DIRECTIONS

Go 12 km south from Salmon Arm on Highway 97B; turn left on Grandview Bench Road for 5.5 km and then left onto Edgar Road about 3 km to a road junction. Take the left fork about 3 km to a parking lot.

DESCRIPTION

The Larch Hills, which are a Provincial Forest, are located on the V-shaped piece of land between the Salmon Arm of Shuswap Lake and the waters of Shuswap River—Mara Lake. The forest is crisscrossed by a network of logging roads both old and new, providing excellent snow-covered routes in winter. The Shuswap Outdoors people have completed a 150-km cross-country trail system along these roads and are building a warming hut. Signs on all the routes give the name and degree of difficulty. Trails are interconnected, and can be followed in a great number of combinations, providing variations in length and challenge. Approximately 15 to 20 km are groomed. We recommend that you purchase the map published by Shuswap Outdoors before checking out the Larch Hills network.

WELLS GRAY PROVINCIAL PARK

Base Elevation: 1000 m
Nearest Community: Clearwater, 40 km
Camping or Accommodations: Helmcken Falls Lodge, outside the park entrance; motels in Clearwater; winter camping should be checked with park headquarters

DIRECTIONS

Wells Gray Provincial Park is located in the Cariboo Mountains, 384 km northeast of Vancouver. Follow Yellowhead Highway 5 north of Kamloops 120 km to the town of Clearwater. Just east of the town is a road leading 40 km north to the park. Park headquarters is now at North Thompson Park, 3 km south of Clearwater on the Yellowhead. In winter, check for road conditions at headquarters before proceeding into the park.

DESCRIPTION

Wells Gray Provincial Park is a 525 980-ha wilderness reserve, a spectacular region of extinct volcanoes, extensive icefields, unclimbed mountains, wild rivers and towering waterfalls. Its remote corners have been visited by only a handful of men, and its rivers were undiscovered until this century. Many people canoe and hike the park in summer, but it was trappers like John Ray and Mike Majerus who cut trapping trails into the more remote regions and first homesteaded the area.

Few other people have seen the park in winter, for only in recent years has the road been kept open as far as Helmcken Falls. Before that it was the snowshoers and skiers who made the trek to see the white volcano that the falls resembles in winter. For ski tourers not requiring prepared trails, there are many areas to consider here, such as the Majerus homestead, Green Mountain, or even Clearwater Lake, but none will equal the spectacular beauty of Helmcken Falls.

Helmcken Falls Lodge, which is located just outside the park entrance, offers some facilities for the cross-country skier. There is a full service ski shop, instruction for beginning skiers, a small store, gas, motel, cabins and licensed dining room. Other winter activities there include snowshoeing, ice fishing and tobogganing.

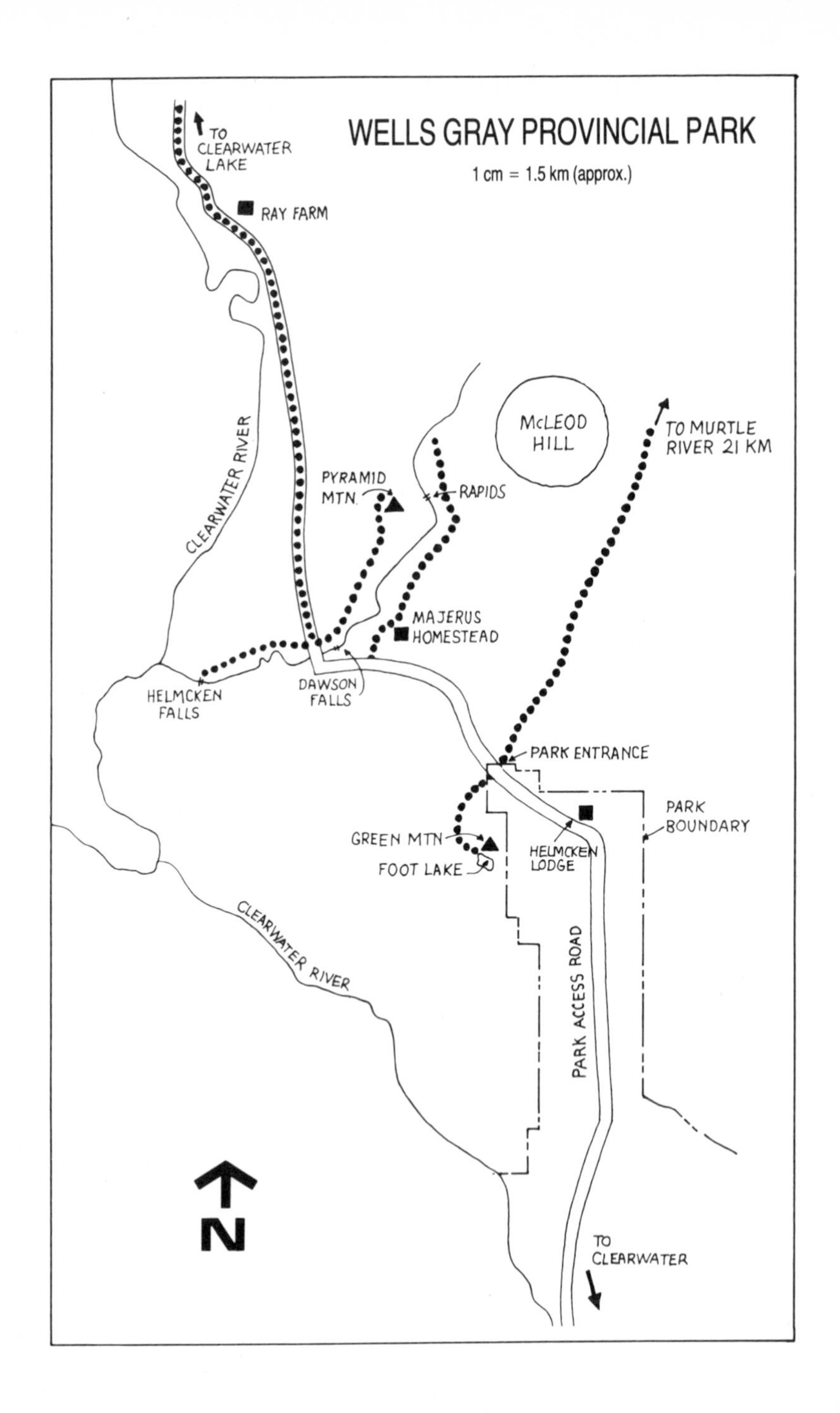
WELLS GRAY PROVINCIAL PARK
1 cm = 1.5 km (approx.)
TO CLEARWATER LAKE
RAY FARM
CLEARWATER RIVER
McLEOD HILL
TO MURTLE RIVER 21 KM
PYRAMID MTN.
RAPIDS
MAJERUS HOMESTEAD
HELMCKEN FALLS
DAWSON FALLS
PARK ENTRANCE
PARK BOUNDARY
GREEN MTN
FOOT LAKE
HELMCKEN LODGE
CLEARWATER RIVER
PARK ACCESS ROAD
N
TO CLEARWATER

GREEN MOUNTAIN TRAIL

Level of Difficulty: Intermediate
Return Length: 6.5 km
Vertical Drop: Approximately 300 m

The Green Mountain Trail follows a summer road that leads to the top of the 300-m mountain or ridge. The road is on the west, or left, side of the park road, a short distance from the actual park entrance sign and the former headquarters area.

From the park road the trail climbs to the top of the ridge in a series of meandering switchbacks through heavy woods. Along the way there is a right fork which leads to the White Horse Bluffs and the Murtle River. (This trail is about 10 km return length, but its suitability for skiing is unknown at present.) For the Green Mountain Trail continue along the left fork, reached at about the halfway point.

At the top of the ridge there is a fine view of the Murtle plateau. Pyramid Mountain may be seen to the northeast, and with a good vantage point on a stump Mahood Lake can be seen to the west, across Clearwater River. Battle Mountain is east and the Trophy Mountains lie just south of Battle. Green Mountain, particularly the west and south sides, is heavily used by moose during winter months. Watch for their tracks along the road.

About 15 minutes' climb from the top of the mountain is Foot Lake. This small lake lies 18 m below the summit of the trail and is reached by a narrow trail that starts just to the right of where you enter the clearing. The trail may be difficult on skis.

MAJERUS HOMESTEAD TRAIL

Level of Difficulty: Beginner to Intermediate
Return Length: 5 km to 21 km
Vertical Drop: Negligible

The trail to the Majerus homestead leaves the park road at 40 km, about 0.5 km south of the Dawson Falls lookout.

This short, easy and pleasant trail leads to the homestead of Mike Majerus on the Murtle River. Majerus came into the area in 1911, working with R. H. Lee who first surveyed the Clearwater Valley. A short time later he built these cabins on the south bank of the Murtle River. The trail is actually an old wagon road that was used in later years as a trail for heavy equipment which had to ford the river rather than take the old Murtle River bridge. It is easily skied by beginners. Those who want to ski a little farther can continue past the farm on the same track.

A short distance upstream of the cabins take the right fork, away from the river. About 2.5 km from the cabins you will reach Pyramid Rapids, a section of river that flows over an old lava outcrop. The trail continues 2.5 km and ends at the Murtle River. The total return distance, from the road to the end of the trail at the river, is approximately 21 km, a more Intermediate trail than the simple glide to the homestead.

PYRAMID MOUNTAIN TRAIL

Level of Difficulty: Beginner to Intermediate
Return Length: 14 km
Vertical Drop: Negligible except for cone, 224 m

The trail to Pyramid Mountain starts on the north side of the Murtle River bridge, at the top of the road's climb out of the river. A sign usually marks the trail. After crossing a bulldozer track and an older trail head, the present trail leads upstream along Murtle River. A short diversion may be made to view Dawson Falls before turning from the river and heading across the plateau towards the old volcanic cone. After breaking out of the trees the track leads across an open burn area,

broken up with a few groves of spruce and cedar. In about an hour you will be at the base of the cone, where the regular trail leading to the Murtle River in summer crosses a flank and begins to climb. Leave the trail here and begin an ascent of the cone. It is approximately 244 m but an easy spiralling trail may be cut. If the weather is fair you will have a view of some of the majestic mountains of Wells Gray, particularly the 3000-m peaks on the north side of Azure Lake. Southeast you will be able to see Battle Mountain and the Trophy Mountains, and to the southwest perhaps the spray of Helmcken Falls, 8 km away. The cone you are standing on erupted about 11 000 years ago.

From here you can simply return to the main road or follow up the trail a little farther. If you follow the trail, in about half an hour you will come to a left fork to the small Pyramid Lakes, which are just a few minutes off the main trail, adding about 3 km to your trip. Caribou and moose are sometimes seen in this area during winter.

Directions should be easily followed. Should you become confused remember that the Murtle River is south of the Pyramid and the road is downstream on the Murtle.

HELMCKEN FALLS TRAIL

Level of Difficulty: Beginner to Intermediate
Return Length: 8 km from park road; 22 km from park entrance
Vertical Drop: Negligible

This trail is actually a road to the viewing point for spectacular Helmcken Falls and lies 7 km north of the park entrance. Usually the road will be open this far, but if not it will be necessary to ski from the park entrance. Even if the road to the falls is plowed it would be an excellent idea to park at the park road and ski the last few kilometres to the falls. It will probably be possible to ski on the road, although sanding or bare spots may mean having to cut a roadside track.

For the 4 km distance to the falls the road follows the north bank of the Murtle River, and many fine winter scenes will be discovered by a winter photographer. As the road nears the parking lot area, swing through the trees to the left, along the canyon rim trail. Be sure to remain behind the barrier. Do *not* ski near the edge of the canyon.

The falls are most awe-inspiring in winter, for though the flow of water is less spectacular, the spray gradually freezes, forming a cone of ice towering many metres above the plunge pool of the falls. It often reaches well above 30 m, and in very cold winters is reported to reach almost to the brink of the falls. Sometime in March it begins to thaw, eventually crashing into the bottom of the canyon.

Watch for wildlife along the road, particularly caribou and moose as well as smaller mammals.

McLEOD HILL TRAIL

Level of Difficulty: Beginner to Advanced
Return Length: 26 km
Vertical Drop: 458 m

This trail starts at the north end of the service compound at the park entrance. Most of the route is along a little-used road that should make fine skiing. McLeod Hill is not suggested as a destination point, but rather as a trail to take for a varying distance, depending on the skier's skill, physical condition and time available. A beginner might be happy to spend an hour on the route while an advanced tourer may want to go as far as McLeod Hill, or beyond, on an overnight trip. The trail actually goes as far as Murtle Lake, another 21 km, though this trek is only for experienced and well-equipped skiers.

The trail winds across a couple of creeks and through some lightly wooded areas on the Murtle Plateau. The road ends near McLeod Hill. The elevation gain is very gradual except for a couple of dips into creek gullies. As in most areas of the park, watch for moose, caribou that have come down from the highlands, and a pack of wolves that frequents the area.

CLEARWATER LAKE TRAIL

Level of Difficulty: Intermediate
Return Length: 45 km from Helmcken Road; 61 km from park entrance
Vertical Drop: Approximately 30 m

This trail follows the park access road, which in most previous winters has been plowed only as far as the Helmcken turnoff. If so, this would be the starting point. Should a heavy snowfall take place the road may only be cleared to the park entrance, so the starting point would be 16 km south. Be sure that park officials know you are touring if you decide to stay overnight. There may be a snowfall that would block the road.

The trail or road generally follows the river to its outlet from Clearwater Lake at Osprey Falls. Along the way the road gains little elevation but does climb and descend in a few locations.

At 11 km it passes the Ray Farm, the former home of John Bunyan Ray and his family who homesteaded there from about 1911. The buildings should not be used for winter shelter because of the danger of collapsing roof timbers.

You pass Shadow Lake 6.5 km beyond the farm and then make a short climb to a ridge. Five km later you cross Falls Creek and arrive at Clearwater campsite. Osprey Falls is located here, and the summer boat launch area is another 2.5 km along the lake. This lake is large and deep with a heavy flow of water; use extreme caution on the ice.

Only experienced skiers with a knowledge of winter survival skills should attempt this trail. Those planning an overnight visit must be adequately equipped for all emergencies. It is very unlikely you will see anyone else, and there is only one direction to go for help. All garbage, of course, should be packed out of this wilderness region.

KAMLOOPS AREA

Level of Difficulty: Beginner to Advanced
Base Elevation: 340 m
Nearest Community: All trails are in Kamloops area
Camping or Accommodations: Kamloops
Map: Individual resort or trail system maps, or Outdoor Recreation Council Map #4, Greater Kamloops Region

DIRECTIONS

Kamloops can be reached along the Trans-Canada Highway or by airline.

DESCRIPTION

The Kamloops area is ideal for cross-country skiing, as is evidenced by the growing number of touring centres and trails. As well, most of the downhill areas are now incorporating cross-country trails into their development. The frequent good snow conditions just above the valley offer skiers many kilometres of roads and trails suitable for lengthy tours. One such area is the Lac du Bois grasslands, north of the city in the Batchelor Hills. It is reached through North Kamloops. Much of the area is closed to vehicles, making it more suitable for skiers. The three downhill areas also have some cross-country trails.

GRANDVIEW ACRES SKI TRAILS

Level of Difficulty: Beginner
Base Elevation: 900 m
Length: 5 km total

Part of a downhill area, these trails are reached 11 km south of Kamloops on the Knutsford Road.

HARPER MOUNTAIN TRAILS

Level of Difficulty: Beginner to Intermediate
Base Elevation: 1250 m
Length: 14 km total

This area is located 24 km from Kamloops on Paul Lake Road. The trails are developed around a downhill area above Paul Lake on the north side of Harper Mountain.

TOD MOUNTAIN

Level of Difficulty: Beginner to Advanced
Length: 25 km total

This development is 53 km from Kamloops on Heffley Creek Road. The trails are part of one of B.C.'s best downhill areas, known for its long runs.

BUSH LAKE SKI TRAILS

Level of Difficulty: Beginner to Advanced
Base Elevation: 1130 m
Length: Network of more than 33 km
Vertical Drop: 450 m
Nearest Community: Kamloops, 19 km
Camping or Accommodations: Kamloops

DIRECTIONS

Turn south off Highway 1, 8 km west of Kamloops; go 11 km along the side road. Timber Lake trails and Bush Lake trails are on the west side of the road for approximately the next 7 km.

DESCRIPTION

Development of the Bush Lake ski trails on crown land has been a co-operative venture between the Ministry of Forests and the Ministry of Lands, Parks and Housing. The routes follow old back roads, meandering through hilly country and around several small lakes. Trails are

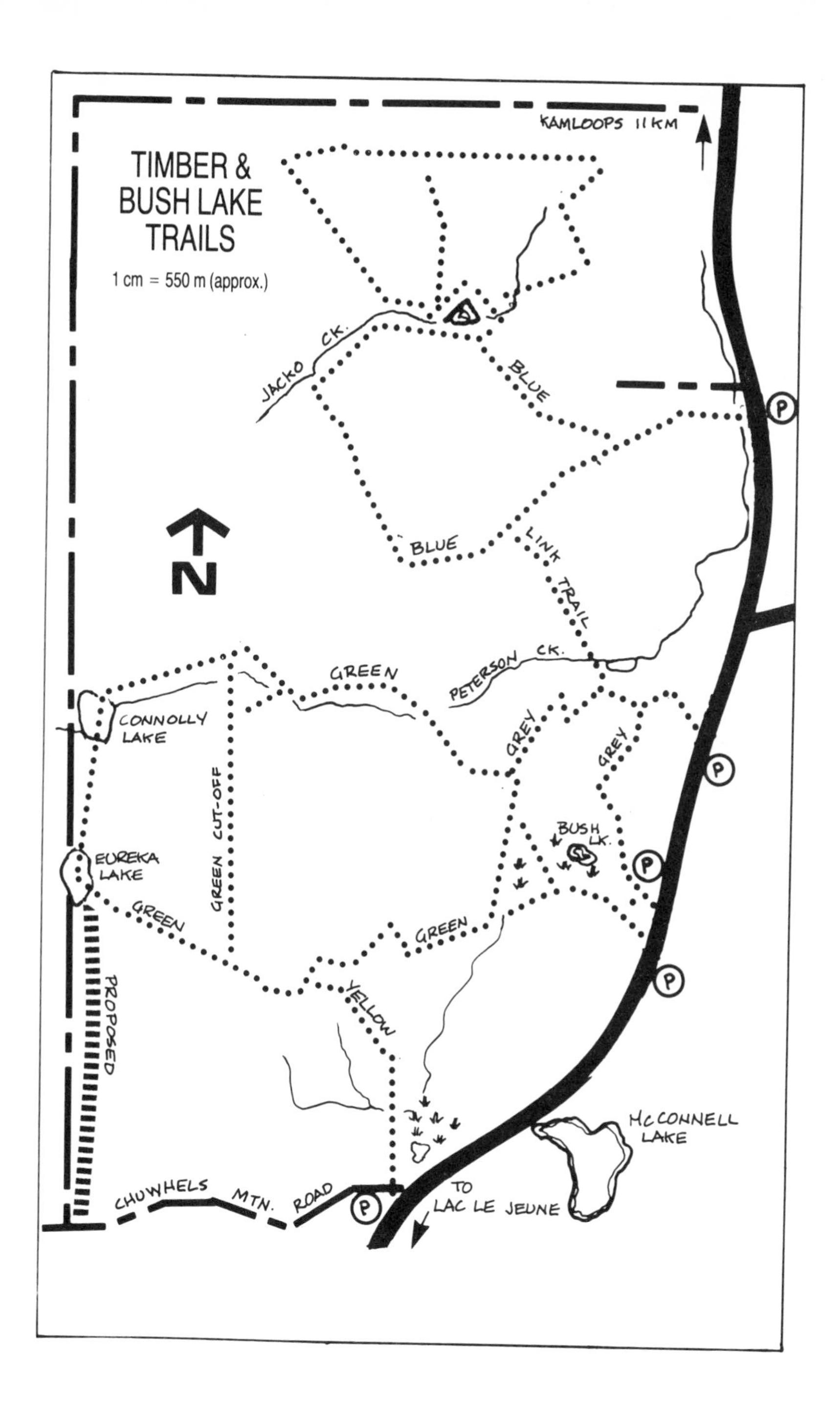
TIMBER & BUSH LAKE TRAILS
1 cm = 550 m (approx.)
KAMLOOPS 11 KM
JACKO CK.
BLUE
BLUE
LINK TRAIL
N
GREEN
PETERSON CK.
CONNOLLY LAKE
GREY
GREY
GREEN CUT-OFF
BUSH LK.
EUREKA LAKE
GREEN
GREEN
YELLOW
PROPOSED
McCONNELL LAKE
CHUWHELS MTN. ROAD
TO LAC LE JEUNE

graded according to difficulty and marked with colour-coded signs posted at 1-km intervals. Skiers are requested to remain on marked trails, as much of the surrounding land is privately owned. Skiers should also use the four designated parking areas at the various access points.

LE JEUNE RESORT NETWORK

Level of Difficulty: Beginner to Advanced
Length: 2 km to 40 km; more than 100 km total
Nearest Community: Kamloops, 37 km
Camping or Accommodations: Le Jeune Lodge and cottages; Kamloops
Map: Available at Le Jeune Lodge

DIRECTIONS

Turn south off Highway 1 at 8 km west of Kamloops; follow the side road 29 km to Lac le Jeune.

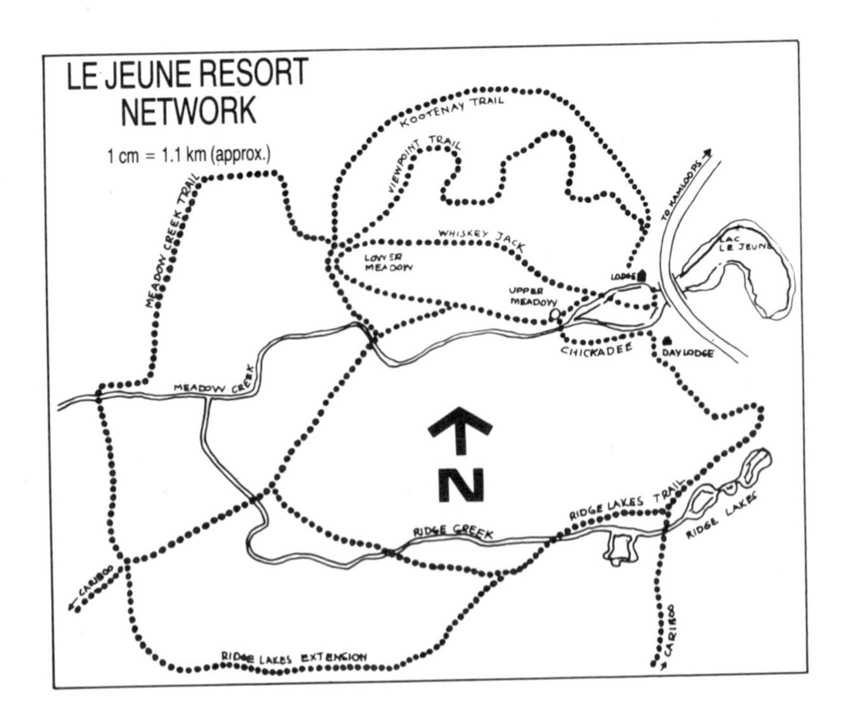

DESCRIPTION

The marked and groomed cross-country trails at Le Jeune Resort are in rolling ranch country. Most of the trails are one-way, so that your return is by a different route. Several can be taken in sequence to make tours of varying length and difficulty. A small fee is charged for use of the trails.

Large groups should make reservations at the lodge well in advance. There is dining and dancing in the Ridge Room, which not only overlooks the lake but also has a massive fireplace hand built with natural stone as an attraction. Also at the resort are facilities for downhill skiing, ice skating, snowshoeing, swimming and a sauna. Since the lodge has recently changed ownership, it would be a good idea to give them a call before heading into the area. Telephone (604) 372-2722.

KANE VALLEY—MENZIES' LOOP

Level of Difficulty: Beginner to Intermediate
Base Elevation: 1125 m
Return Length: 15-km loop
Vertical Drop: 50 m
Nearest Community: Merritt, 18 km
Camping or Accommodations: Nearby lodges and Merritt
Map: Trail map available from Ministry of Forests, Merritt

DIRECTIONS

The Kane Valley, 18 km south of Merritt, has three cross-country areas. The first is found at km 1.8 on the Kane Valley Road, off Highway 5.

DESCRIPTION

Menzies' Loop is about a three-hour ski, winding through open country west of the Kane Valley Road. It was constructed and is maintained by local enthusiasts and the Ministry of Forests. The area has a good snowfall, unlike the lower Merritt Valley, and is not subject to the warm winds that melt snow in the Aspen Grove area.

KANE VALLEY—MATTHEW'S LOOP

Level of Difficulty: Beginner to Intermediate
Base Elevation: 1125 m
Return Length: 5 km
Vertical Drop: 100 m
Nearest Community: Merritt, 20 km
Camping or Accommodations: Nearby lodges and Merritt
Map: Trail map available from Ministry of Forests, Merritt

DIRECTIONS

The Kane Valley lies 18 km south of Merritt. This loop is located at km 3.7 on Kane Valley Road off Highway 5.

DESCRIPTION

This loop trail is named for Matthew Howes, a skiing enthusiast from Merritt. The trail begins on the south side of the Kane Valley Road and follows a path through open woods and meadows. Follow this trail in a clockwise direction to take advantage of the grades. It ends with a short steep climb and a long descent to an old log dump.

KANE VALLEY—ROBINSON'S LOOP

Level of Difficulty: Intermediate
Base Elevation: 1125 m
Return Length: Approximately 5 km
Vertical Drop: 150 m
Nearest Community: Merritt, 20 km
Camping or Accommodations: Nearby lodges and Merritt
Map: Trail map available from Ministry of Forests, Merritt

DIRECTIONS

The third loop in the Kane Valley, this trail is reached from km 3.7 or km 6 on Kane Valley Road.

DESCRIPTION

This series of loops allows skiers to vary the distance they wish to ski. All the trails are on old logging roads and some of the grades require a certain amount of downhill skill. The loops swing south of the Kane Lakes and connect with Matthew's Loop.

KOOTENAY REGION

The mountains of the Kootenays include the Selkirks, the Purcells and the Rockies. Many of the cross-country trails are adapted from hiking trails in alpine regions. Others follow old logging and mining roads. The season here tends to be longer than in the Lower Mainland, usually from November to May.

MOUNT REVELSTOKE NATIONAL PARK

Mount Revelstoke National Park lies at the western side of the Selkirk Mountains and overlooks the town of Revelstoke on the Columbia River. The Selkirks are distinguished from the Rockies by their narrow peaks and greater age. This large area of rugged mountain terrain was established as a national park in 1914. It is a region of heavy precipitation with winter snowfall averaging 9 m to 12 m or more.

Base Elevation: 600 m
Nearest Community: Revelstoke, 4 km
Camping or Accommodations: Shelters along Mount Revelstoke Road for overnight camping; Revelstoke

DIRECTIONS

Access to the park is on the north side of Highway 1 at Revelstoke. Start up the Mount Revelstoke Road and then turn right on Ski Hill Road and continue about 1 km to the parking lot. For the Mount Revelstoke Route, stay on Mount Revelstoke Road.

REVELSTOKE SKI CLUB TRAILS

Return Length: 2 km and 5 km
Map: Revelstoke Ski Club map available from local outdoor stores

Two marked trails are kept groomed by the Revelstoke Ski Club, Cross-Country Division, and are generally in good condition considering the quantities of snow the club has to deal with. The trails begin at the Mount Revelstoke cross-country ski hut just beyond the National Park interchange east of town.

MOUNT REVELSTOKE ROAD

Return Length: 52 km
Vertical Drop: Approximately 1400 m
Map: Park brochure with the road marked on it available from Parks Canada

Mount Revelstoke Road is closed in winter from approximately 1 km beyond the turnoff to the ski area. The roadbed from there to the summit of Mount Revelstoke is used by both skiers and snowmobilers. The 26-km road is a series of switchbacks winding steeply up the mountain, with many viewpoints on the way of surrounding mountains, such as Big Eddy of the Columbia, Eagle Pass, Illecillewaet Valley and the mountain burg of Revelstoke. The summit of Mount Revelstoke is rolling alpine hills. There are winter shelters located at 8 km, 19.4 km and 24 km along the road. All skiers staying out overnight must register with the Warden Service at the park office between the hours of 8 A.M. and 4:30 P.M., Monday to Friday.

REVELSTOKE SKI TRAILS

Level of Difficulty: Beginner to Advanced
Base Elevation: 457 m
Nearest Community: All trails are in Revelstoke area
Camping or Accommodations: Revelstoke
Map: Revelstoke Ski Club map available from local outdoor stores

DIRECTIONS

Revelstoke is located on the Trans-Canada Highway and can be reached by CP Rail, bus lines and car.

DESCRIPTION

The club map shows 12 good trails in the surrounding area. La Forme Creek, 23 km north of Revelstoke, is 8 km long with an initial steep section of 2 km. It ends at an old mining settlement. Frisbee Ridge is an

8-km trail that begins at the end of a logging road. Wap Creek is a logging road system 23 km west of town. Others are indicated on the map. Some are more suited to touring.

MOUNT MacPHERSON SKI AREA

Level of Difficulty: Beginner to Intermediate
Base Elevation: 580 m
Length: 25-km network
Vertical Drop: 520 m
Nearest Community: Revelstoke, 6 km
Camping or Accommodations: Revelstoke
Map: Revelstoke Ski Club map available from local outdoor stores

DIRECTIONS

The Mount MacPherson ski area is located 6 km south of Revelstoke on Highway 23 on the Mica-Nakusp Road.

DESCRIPTION

This cross-country area has been developed by the Ministry of Forests and the Revelstoke Ski Club. It consists of several loops which climb above the highway to the west. One goes to Beaver Lake, another loops for 7 km and another climbs higher in a 14-km loop.

GLACIER NATIONAL PARK

Glacier National Park is located in the middle of the Selkirk Mountains and has more than 100 glaciers within its boundaries. It is the oldest national park in Canada. The park offers several fine ski touring areas in a wilderness setting. The area is subject to heavy snowfalls and the trails are not groomed or packed. A knowledge of ski mountaineering procedures is essential here and sturdy equipment is advisable.

There are some restrictions on winter outdoor activities in Glacier, because of the avalanche hazard and the need to keep transportation routes open. Several areas are completely closed to public travel during the avalanche season. Check with the park administration for more details on these closed areas. The Snow Research and Avalanche Warning Section of Parks Canada is responsible for the forecast and control of avalanches in the Rogers Pass, and uses artillery fire for snow stabilization. Parking within the park is allowed only in plowed areas alongside the highway. When an avalanche control program is being carried out, a red card is put on the windshields of cars in the area; it is most important that vehicles marked in this way not be moved until an official indicates that it is safe to do so.

All ski tourers *must* register at the Park Administration Building at Rogers Pass, or at the Northlander Lodge if staying there. Registration is also necessary for staying at the Wheeler Hut.

Northlander Motor Lodge at the summit of Rogers Pass operates a cafeteria and gas station and offers accommodations.

Because of the heavy annual snowfall, which averages about 8.7 m, few large mammals inhabit Glacier Park. The bears that do live there will not be seen in winter months.

Nearest Communities: Golden, 80 km east; Revelstoke, 68 km west
Camping or Accommodations: Northlander Motor Lodge at Rogers Pass; Revelstoke
Map: Park ski touring brochure available from Glacier National Park headquarters or from Parks Canada, Ottawa

DIRECTIONS

Take Highway 1 east from Revelstoke 48 km to the western entrance of Glacier National Park; it is another 38 km along the highway to the eastern end of Glacier.

LOWER BEAVER VALLEY

Although there are no trails here, there is a good flat area suitable for skiing in the Mountain Creek campground and along the Beaver River upstream from Mountain Creek. Travel is mostly through woods but glimpses of surrounding peaks can be seen between the trees.

BEAVER RIVER TRAIL

Return Length: Approximately 84 km

This trail leaves the highway about 13.7 km east of Rogers Pass summit and follows the Beaver River to its headwaters by way of an easy grade

and some short climbs. The trail forks at about 6.4 km; keep to the right to cross Grizzly Creek and continue up the Beaver. Most of the trail is through woods.

COPPERSTAIN TRAIL

Return Length: Approximately 42 km

Copperstain Trail begins as the Beaver River Trail and forks to the left at 6.4 km. It follows Grizzly Creek for 3.2 km and then Copperstain Creek into the Bald Hills. The trail climbs through woods until the open areas of the Bald Hills are reached.

ASULKAN & ILLECILLEWAET AREAS

Parking for the next four trails is at the bottom of Glacier Hill south of the highway across from the hotel gun position. To reach the trail area, climb up to the railway grade and along it to the area behind Illecillewaet campground. Do not use the summer road as it passes through the critical avalanche area of Avalanche Crest.

MARION LAKE TRAIL

Return Length: Approximately 4.8 km

Marion Lake Trail is a steep switchback route up the mountain from Illecillewaet campground to Marion Lake. At the lake you will have a good view of the Illecillewaet Valley. Above the lake is an avalanche area. Skis with climbing skins or climbing wax are needed on this route.

ASULKAN TRAIL

Return Length: 12.8 km

This trail leads up Asulkan Glacier from behind the Illecillewaet campground. It is fairly flat, with a gradual grade, and leads through dense woods for 4.8 km, then more open woods.

ILLECILLEWAET TRAIL

Return Length: 6.4 km

Leading to the headwaters of the Illecillewaet River, the trail follows an easy grade through dense woods until an avalanche area is reached and the glacier can be seen.

AVALANCHE CREST TRAIL

Return Length: 11.2 km

The Avalanche Crest Trail is steep and zigzags up the east slope of the valley from the Wheeler Hut to the crest. This route provides scenic views of valleys, peaks and glaciers. There is a critical avalanche area to the right of the trail on the crest which should be avoided. Climbing skins or climbing wax are necessary.

BOSTOCK CREEK TRAIL

Return Length: 16 km

West of Rogers Pass about 19 km, Bostock Creek Trail heads north from the highway up the east side of Bostock Creek. It passes through dense forest and crosses several avalanche paths. Skiers should not travel beyond the pass into Casualty Creek.

MOONRAKER NETWORK

Level of Difficulty: Beginner to Advanced
Length: 35-km network
Vertical Drop: 270 m
Nearest Community: Golden, 12 km
Camping or Accommodations: Motels and hotels at Golden
Map: A detailed map of the cross-country trails of the area has been published on waterproof paper and is available from Golden Outdoors Club, P.O. Box 2190, Golden, B.C. V0A 1H0

DIRECTIONS

Go south from Golden on Highway 95 approximately 6 km to Nicholson; a side road to the right crosses a bridge over the Columbia River and then continues another 6 km to the Moonraker parking lot.

DESCRIPTION

The Moonraker network of trails is located on a glacial bench between the Dogtooth Range of the Purcell Mountains and the Columbia River. The trails wind across rolling hills past small lakes and across frozen streams. The individual trails are marked according to difficulty and range in length from 0.1 km to 5.3 km. They can be taken in many different sequences according to the level of difficulty desired and the time available. The waterproof map, which includes brief descriptions of the trails, would be a valuable asset in planning ski tours of the area. Panoramic views are the attraction of many of these routes.

MOUNT ASSINIBOINE PROVINCIAL PARK

Level of Difficulty: Advanced
Return Length: 54.6 km
Nearest Community: Banff, 24 km from the start of the trail at Sunshine Ski Village
Camping or Accommodations: Naiset cabins on the east side of Lake Magog; Mt. Assiniboine Lodge; Banff
Map: Park pamphlet available from the Ministry of Lands, Parks and Housing, Parks and Outdoor Recreation Division; contour map (1:25 000) and National Topographic Series maps (1:50 000) available from Ministry of Environment, Survey and Resource Mapping Branch

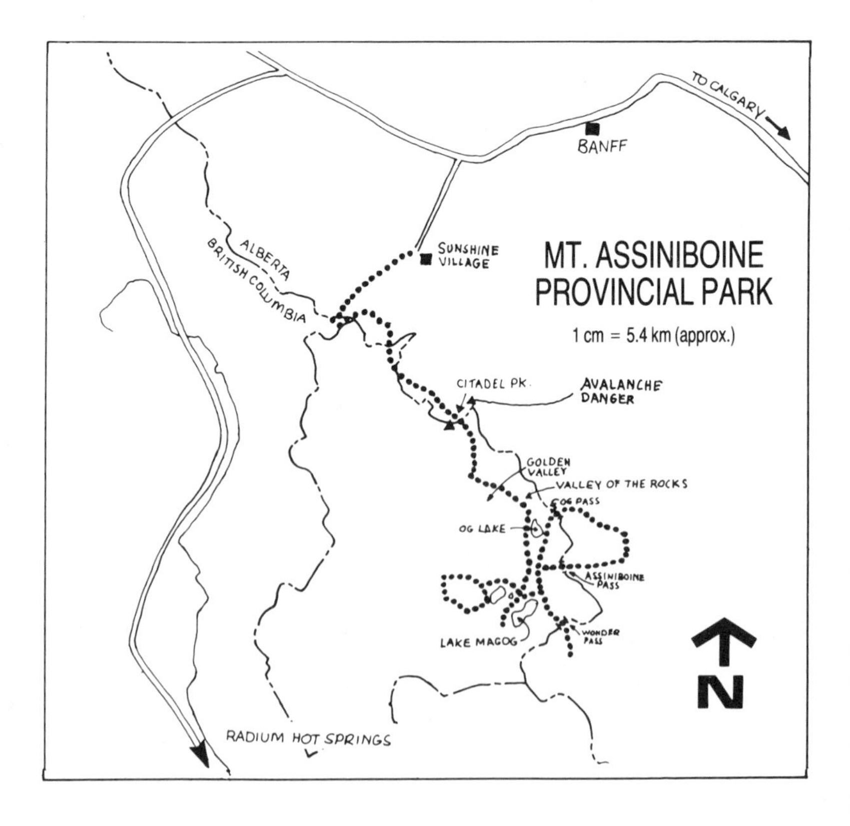

DIRECTIONS

Go west 9.6 km from Banff, then follow the Sunshine Ski Village access road 8.8 km to the Bourgeau parking lot. Then either take the scheduled bus or ski 5.6 km to the resort and take the trail head to Lake Magog.

DESCRIPTION

Mount Assiniboine, a peak in the Rocky Mountains which looks something like the Swiss Matterhorn, was named after the Indians who hunted in this area. The triangular park, which is named for the mountain, is wedged between Banff National Park to the east and Kootenay National Park in the west. There are no roads into Mount Assiniboine Provincial Park; the only access is by trails.

The main access route for skiers is from the Sunshine Ski area in Banff National Park, via Citadel Pass and the Valley of the Rocks. This route is very difficult and demanding. Parks Branch personnel advise that it should not be attempted by inexperienced or improperly equipped skiers.

Since the south side of Citadel is avalanche prone, and skiers tend to get lost in the Valley of the Rocks when they try to follow the lay of the land, Parks Branch suggests the following route: "From the bottom of Citadel Pass, traverse around the toe of a large avalanche fan which is situated on the south side of the pass, then climb up along the southern edge of the slide to a rock outcropping and then traverse southerly to another outcropping; staying on the uphill side, traverse at a steady uphill grade just inside the trees for approximately 4 km, then angle into the centre of the valley and follow the natural clearings to Og Lake. Beware of a large avalanche slope which crosses the valley just before Og Lake. Stay well up on the opposite (west) slope."

From Lake Magog there are several day trips that can be taken in the area.

Skiers going into Assiniboine should register with the park warden at the Sunshine Ski area, and have topographical maps of the park. Also read the daily avalanche hazard bulletin and be prepared to camp out overnight. April and early May are the best times to make this trip, since the avalanche danger is not as great as in the winter months.

Some helicopter access into the park is being allowed by the Parks Branch on an experimental basis. For information contact Helicopter Pilot, P.O. Box 1031, Banff, Alberta, T0L 0C0; (403) 762-4082.

FAIRMONT HOT SPRINGS

Base Elevation: 850 m
Nearest Community: Golden, 138 km
Camping or Accommodations: Lodging at Fairmont Hot Springs Resort
Map: Available from Fairmont Hot Springs Resort

DIRECTIONS

Go 138 km south from Golden on Highway 93/95.

DESCRIPTION

A popular resort and convention centre, Fairmont Hot Springs is located on the western slopes of the Rocky Mountains. In winter there are 16 km of ski touring trails as well as downhill facilities, helicopter skiing and a hang gliding ski program. Cross-country rentals and instruction are available and there is a ski patrol.

The main attraction of the resort is the hot pools (35–42° C)—a special treat to come back to after a day of skiing. At the ski area are a chalet, licensed cafeteria and ski shop; the lodge facilities include varied mod-

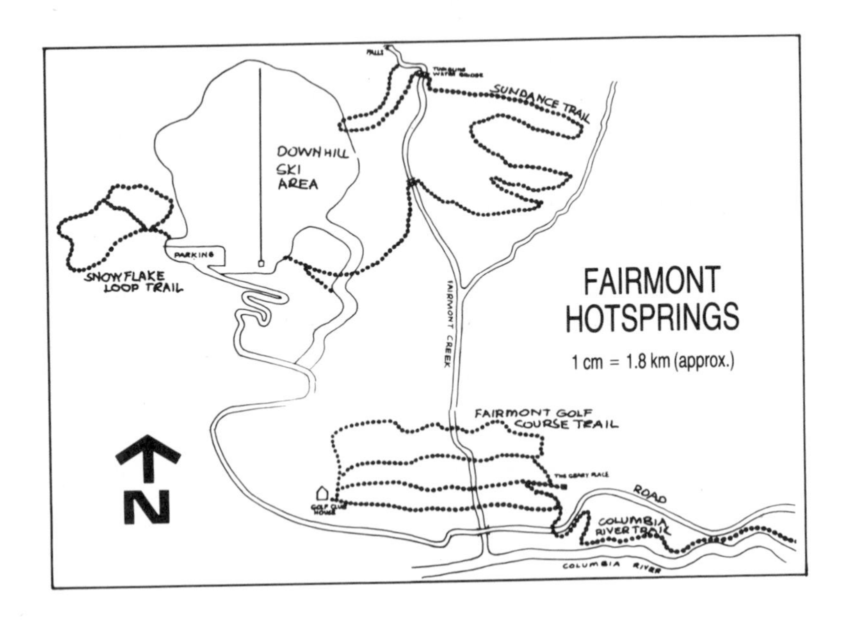

ern accommodations, pools, saunas, dining lounge, coffee shop and entertainment. Special *après ski* activities include Gluhwein, cheese fondues and horse-drawn hayrides.

SNOWFLAKE LOOP TRAIL

Level of Difficulty: Beginner
Length: 0.8 km

This trail begins near the parking lot at the downhill ski area. It meanders through flat and gently rolling terrain, protected from winds by the tall fir and tamarack trees under which it passes. The trail can be done in about 15 minutes.

SUNDANCE TRAIL

Level of Difficulty: Intermediate to Advanced
Return Length: 11.2 km

The Sundance Trail begins from the parking lot on the far side of the downhill ski area. It crosses a ski run and then begins zigzagging gently up the mountain slope through fir and tamarack forest. Along the way are views across the Windermere Valley and of other alpine scenery. The trail crosses Fairmont Creek twice and ends at Fairmont Falls. Rabbits and other small mammals may be seen. Return is by the same trail or, if preferred, down the shorter downhill route from about 0.8 km below the falls.

FAIRMONT GOLF COURSE

Level of Difficulty: Beginner to Advanced
Length: 5.9 km

A series of trails on the smooth open rolling hills of the golf course include the 1–9 Hole Loop of 3.1 km and the 10–18 Hole Loop of 2.9 km. The area is surrounded by beautiful views of the Fairmont Mountains, south to Columbia Lake and across to the Purcell Mountains. The trails begin by the golf clubhouse.

COLUMBIA RIVER TRAIL

Level of Difficulty: Intermediate to Advanced

The open riverbanks along the Columbia River valley provide good ski touring territory. The route can be started across the road from the south end of the golf course and can be followed for any distance desired. A river boat historic site is passed on the river, and many signs of mammals and birds are likely to be seen.

KIMBERLEY SKI RESORT

Level of Difficulty: Beginner, Intermediate, Advanced
Base Elevation: 1280 m
Length: 24-km network
Nearest Community: Kimberley, 2.4 km
Camping or Accommodations: Campground and lodge at the resort; motels in Kimberley
Map: Available from Kimberley Ski Resort

DIRECTIONS

Kimberley Ski Resort is 2.4 km south of Kimberley, which is located on Highway 95A, 32 km north of Cranbrook and 128 km south of Radium Hot Springs.

DESCRIPTION

Though primarily a downhill ski area, the Kimberley Ski Resort on North Star Mountain also has trails and areas for cross-country skiing, snowshoeing, snowmobiling, skating and curling. The school has a cross-country instructor and rental equipment is available. The lodge facilities include a cafeteria, dining room and lounge; and babysitting day or evening can be arranged. The winter campground is complete with electric hookups and showers. The well-marked cross-country trails start at the base of the downhill ski area.

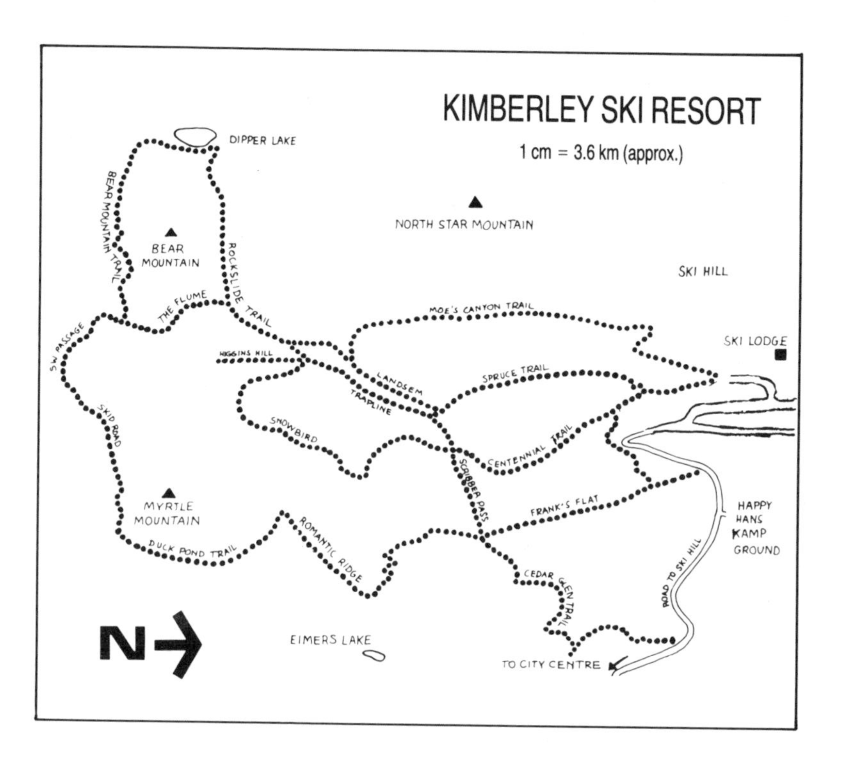

RED MOUNTAIN

Level of Difficulty: Beginner to Advanced
Length: 20 km total, plus alpine
Nearest Community: Rossland, 3.2 km
Camping or Accommodations: Rossland and at ski hill

DIRECTIONS

Rossland is reached via Highway 3B or by air service to Castlegar, then bus.

DESCRIPTION

Red Mountain is an old volcanic cone around which a downhill ski area was begun in 1947 by the Red Mountain Ski Club. The original hand-built chairlift has been replaced by a modern one. Cross-country trails begin at the base of ski lifts or in alpine country. The Granite Mountain area has cross-country trails at the base of the mountain, beginning

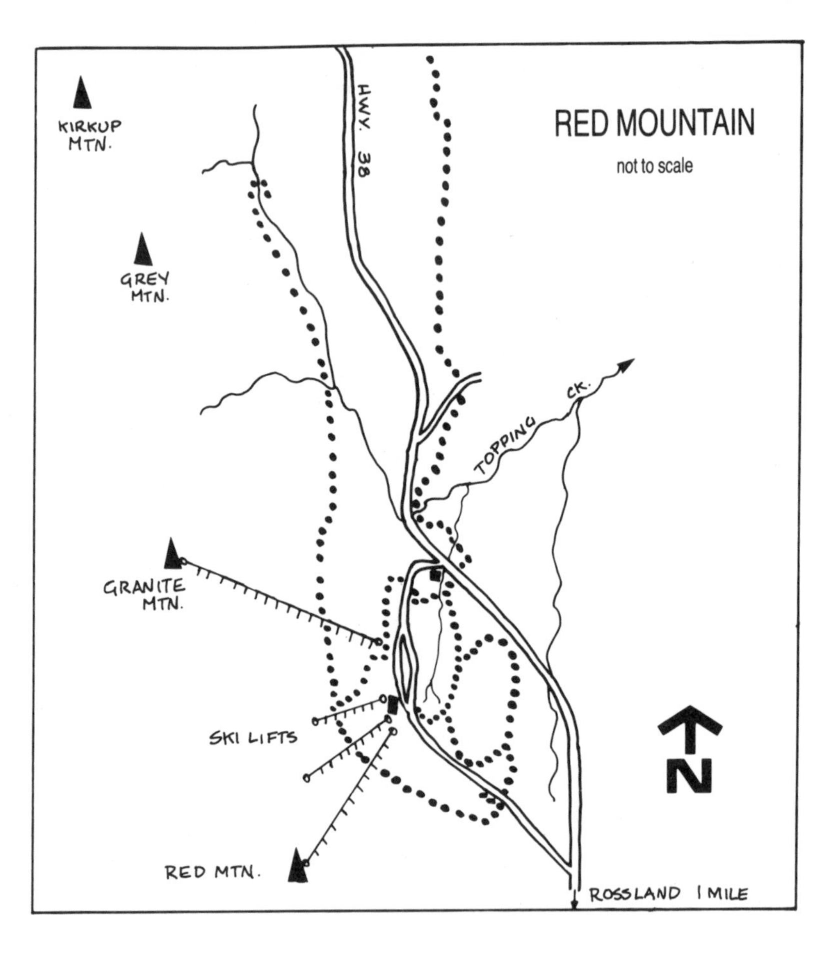

near the lodge. There are also Nordic touring trails to Record Ridge, Grey Mountain and Kirkup Mountain, which can be approached by walking, lifts or helicopter.

PAULSON COUNTRY SKI TRAILS

Level of Difficulty: Beginner to Advanced
Base Elevation: 1250 m
Length: 25-km network
Nearest Communities: Rossland, 23 km; Christina Lake, 45 km; Castlegar, 26 km
Camping or Accommodations: At all of the above communities
Map: Paulson Country Winter Recreation brochure available from Ministry of Lands, Parks and Housing, Parks and Outdoor Recreation Division, 612 Front Street, Nelson, B.C. V1L 4B7

DIRECTIONS

The area is reached on Highway 3 from Castlegar and Christina Lake, or on 3B from Rossland and Trail.

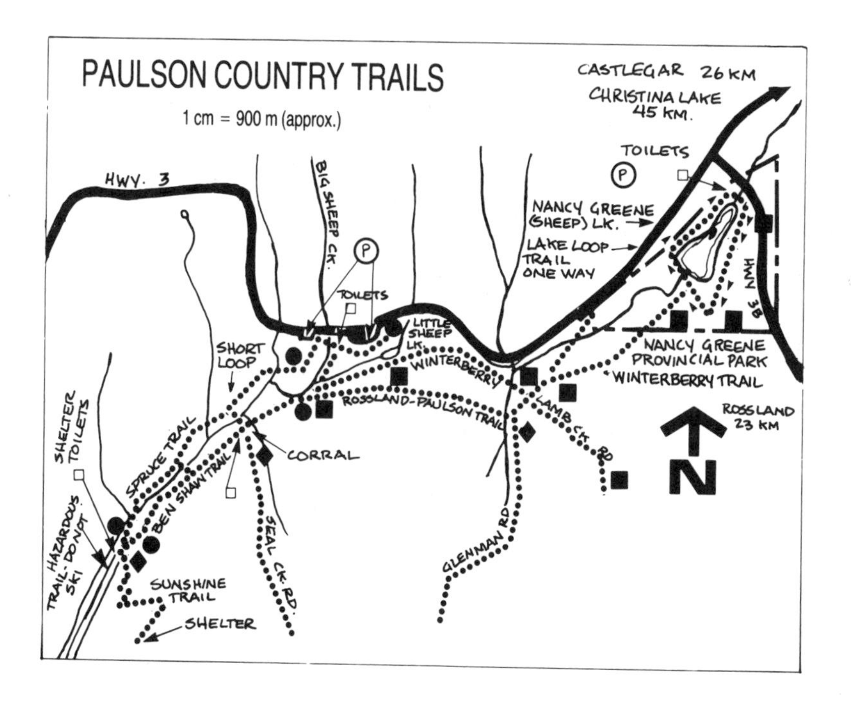

DESCRIPTION

The Paulson Country trails are located in and around Nancy Greene Provincial Park, a 183-ha park at the junction of Highways 3 and 3B. Other trails run west from the park. Some use unplowed roads. The trails that begin near the park entrance are the Lake Loop, an Intermediate trail of 3.2 km return length around Nancy Greene (Sheep) Lake, and the 7.9-km Winterberry Trail, also an Intermediate trail, which provides access to a system of trails maintained by the Ministry of Forests and the Ben Shaw Ski Society. Some shelters have been erected by the society, and there is a parking lot west of the park entrance on Highway 3.

STAGLEAP PROVINCIAL PARK

Level of Difficulty: Beginner to Intermediate
Base Elevation: 1768 m
Length: 2.5 km
Nearest Communities: Salmo, 37 km west; Creston, 45 km east
Camping or Accommodations: At both the above communities
Map: Park brochure available from Ministry of Lands, Parks and Housing, Parks and Outdoor Recreation Division, 612 Front Street, Nelson, B.C. V1L 4B7

DIRECTIONS

The Southern Trans-Canada Highway, Highway 3, passes through the park 37 km east of Salmo and 45 km west of Creston.

DESCRIPTION

This small park is located at the summit of Kootenay Pass in the Selkirk Mountains. A remnant herd of mountain, or woodland, caribou frequent the area and may sometimes be seen. Heavy snowfall means that skiing lasts well into spring.

The two trails here are rather short, but for skiers travelling by car they make a good exercise break. The Caribou Trail is a 1-km loop on the west side of Bridal Lake; the Bridal Lake Trail loops to the north of the lake and is suitable for intermediates.

YOHO NATIONAL PARK

Level of Difficulty: Beginner to Advanced
Return Length: 4 km to 58 km
Nearest Community: Trails centre around Field
Camping or Accommodations: Camping in the park; Field and Golden, B.C. (west), and Banff, Alberta (east)
Map: Ski trail brochure available from park office in Field

DIRECTIONS

The park surrounds the Trans-Canada Highway at Field. Access is by the highway.

DESCRIPTION

Skiers and winter recreationists come to this attractive mountainous park to enjoy winter silence, deep snows and ice waterfalls. There are a total of 15 trails suitable for Nordic skiing. Most are a comfortable length for day touring and some are periodically groomed; the longer ones are more suited for tours of several days. Trails are numbered west to east along the highway.

1. Wapta Falls, Intermediate, 8 km return.
2. Chancellor Peak Campground Road, Beginner, 4 km return along the road.
3. Hoodoo Creek Campground, Beginner, variable loop of 4 km return within campground.
4. Ice River Road, Intermediate, 32 km return. Trail leads south along the Kicking Horse River.
5. Ottertail Fire Road, Intermediate, 32 km return. Trail leads southeast along the Ottertail River. Winter camping at end of road.
6. Amiskwi, Intermediate, 58 km return. Trail runs north along Amiskwi River.
7. Otterhead Fire Road, Beginner, 13 km return.
8. Emerald River, Intermediate, 16 km return. Trail follows river north to Trail 9, Emerald Lake Road; return via Emerald Lake Road if desired.
9. Emerald Lake Road, Beginner, 16 km return. Follows road north to parking lot.
10. Emerald River Road, Intermediate, 9 km return.
11. Emerald Lake Circuit, Intermediate, 21 km return. Combines above three trails in a loop.
12. Takakkaw Falls, Intermediate, 26 km return. Follows the road up the Yoho River to Trail 13.

13. Little Yoho, Advanced, 19-km return trail from Takakkaw Falls. Steep trail with avalanche hazard.
14. Lake O'Hara, Intermediate, 26 km return. Trail leads along the road to the lake. Camping at the lake.
15. Ross Lake Circuit, Intermediate, 9.5 km return.

Consult the Warden Service in the park for more information before taking any of these trails. The number is (604) 343-6467.

KOOTENAY NATIONAL PARK

Level of Difficulty: Beginner to Advanced
Length: 6.4 km to 32 km
Nearest Community: Radium Hot Springs, 2 km west of park entrance
Camping or Accommodations: Camping in the park; accommodations at Radium Hot Springs
Map: Trail guide available from Superintendent, Kootenay National Park, P.O. Box 220, Radium Hot Springs, B.C. V0A 1M0; (604) 347-9615

DIRECTIONS

Kootenay National Park is one of the mountain parks that stretch along the Rocky Mountains. Kootenay lies on the west slope and is about 104 km in length and 15 km wide. Highway 93 runs up the centre and provides access to all park trails.

DESCRIPTION

Kootenay National Park is not promoted specifically as a winter recreation area, yet there are many trails that can be used for ski touring. The Parks Service has suggested Trail 8 as being suitable for most skiers.

1A. Mount Shanks Fire Tower Road, 9.6 km return. Follows the road and climbs about 300 m.
1B. Simpson River, 16 km return. Follows the left riverbank.
2. West Kootenay Fire Road, a loop of 19 km.
3. Hector Gorge, 11.2 km. Trail leaves the highway north of Dolly Varden picnic site and reaches the gorge above Kootenay Ponds.
4. Split Peak, 6.4 km one way. Same access as Hector Gorge.

5. East Kootenay. Follows down the east side of the Kootenay River for varying distances; 32 km return to the Cross River Trail near Nipika Touring Centre.
6. Dolly Varden, 11.2 km return. Loop trail from Kootenay Warden Station or Dolly Varden picnic site. Winter camping at picnic site.
7. Dog Lake, 6.4 km. A short trail for an easy ski. Crosses East Kootenay Trail. Park at McLeod Meadows picnic site.
8. Cross River, 17 km one way. Trail from end of East Kootenay to the Nipika Touring Centre.

INVERMERE-PANORAMA TRAILS

Base Elevation: 1200 m
Return Length: 4 km to 23 km
Nearest Community: Invermere, 17 km
Camping or Accommodations: Panorama Ski Resort and Invermere
Map: Map of Panorama trails available at ski resort; also Outdoor Recreation Council Map #2, Windermere Lake Region

DIRECTIONS

Panorama Ski Resort is reached from Invermere in the Columbia Valley. The resort is 17 km up Toby Creek in the Purcell Mountains. Invermere can be reached by Highway 93/95 or by air to Cranbrook-Kimberley.

DESCRIPTION

Although primarily a downhill resort, Panorama has developed 25 km of cross-country trails in the vicinity. Ski rentals are available. All trails begin at the south end of the resort area. They are signed and groomed but not patrolled.

HOPEFUL BASIN TRAIL

Level of Difficulty: Beginner
Return Length: 4 km

The trail follows Hopeful Creek in a southerly direction through lodgepole pine forests, with a loop across the creek.

LUKE'S RUN TRAIL

Level of Difficulty: Intermediate
Return Length: 4 km

This trail begins on the Hopeful Basin Trail then makes a loop along an outfitter's original pack trail. There is a side trail going to Hopeful Lookout, though it is a little tricky.

WILDWOOD TRAIL

Level of Difficulty: Intermediate
Return Length: 11 km

The Wildwood Trail continues beyond the end of the Hopeful Basin Trail. It drops down to Toby Creek and then climbs to Black Bear Hill. At the Barbour Creek Bridge the trail divides into two loops, the Upper and Lower Delphine loops.

If you are heading away from the lodge, take the upper loop, a one-way trail. There are some switchbacks as you climb to the Mt. Nelson Lookout.

From here you continue on the Lower Delphine Loop for a return to the lodge. This too is one-way and will lead you back to the Wildwood Trail.

DELPHINE CREEK TRAIL

Level of Difficulty: Intermediate
Base Elevation: 1250 m
Return Length: 18 km
Vertical Drop: 600 m
Nearest Community: Invermere, 27 km
Camping or Accommodations: Panorama Ski Resort; Invermere; wildnerness camping
Map: Outdoor Recreation Council Map #2, Windermere Lake Region

DIRECTIONS

The trail begins at the Soda Mineral Spring, 10 km up Toby Creek from Panorama Ski Resort. Watch for the trail head on the right side of the road.

DESCRIPTION

The trail follows Delphine Creek upstream on the right side. A view of the Delphine Icefall on the left is worth watching for. There is some avalanche hazard, so travel prepared. Near the end of the trail is a junction where you can fork right or left.

PARADISE MINE TRAIL

Level of Difficulty: Intermediate
Base Elevation: 1100 m
Return Length: 24 km
Vertical Drop: 1180 m
Nearest Community: Invermere, 16 km
Camping or Accommodations: Panorama Ski Resort; Invermere; wilderness camping
Map: Outdoor Recreation Council Map #2, Windermere Lake Region

DIRECTIONS

The trail head is 16 km up the Toby Creek road towards Panorama, on the right.

DESCRIPTION

The 12-km road winding up the mountain above Springs Creek leads to the abandoned Paradise Mine site. This route is also used by snowmobiles but once at the mine you will be surrounded by powder bowls. If you are looking for powder continue towards Watch Peak. There is an avalanche hazard in some areas along this route, so use caution.

SHUSWAP CREEK TRAIL

Level of Difficulty: Intermediate
Base Elevation: 1000 m
Return Length: 23 km
Vertical Drop: 1000 m
Nearest Communities: Invermere, Athalmer and Windermere, 5 km
Camping or Accommodations: At all of the above communities
Map: Outdoor Recreation Council Map #2, Windermere Lake Region

DIRECTIONS

Shuswap Creek Trail is on the east side of the Columbia Valley. To reach the trail head, drive to the Highway 95/93 junction. Almost directly across the highway, on the east side, is the road to Shuswap Creek.

DESCRIPTION

The trail follows the left (north) bank of Shuswap Creek. At the trail end is Kimpton Pass, a long ski for most. Watch for slide dangers.

RADIUM HOT SPRINGS GOLF & COUNTRY CLUB

Level of Difficulty: Beginner to Intermediate
Base Elevation: 900 m
Length: l4-km network
Nearest Community: Radium Hot Springs, 3 km
Camping or Accommodations: On site and in Radium Hot Springs
Map: Available from club pro shop

DIRECTIONS

Club is located 3 km south of Radium Hot Springs on Highway 93/95. The town is serviced by bus lines and is 135 km from Banff, 145 km from Cranbrook.

DESCRIPTION

During the snow season the links of the golf course are set in loops that total 14 km or more. They are open daily; instruction and rentals are available. There is a trail fee.

COLUMBIA VALLEY NORDIC TRAILS

Level of Difficulty: Beginner to Intermediate
Base Elevation: 900 m
Return Length: 50 km
Vertical Drop: 200 m
Nearest Community: Radium Hot Springs, 9 km
Camping or Accommodations: Radium Hot Springs
Map: Trails are shown on Outdoor Recreation Council Map #2, Windermere Lake Region

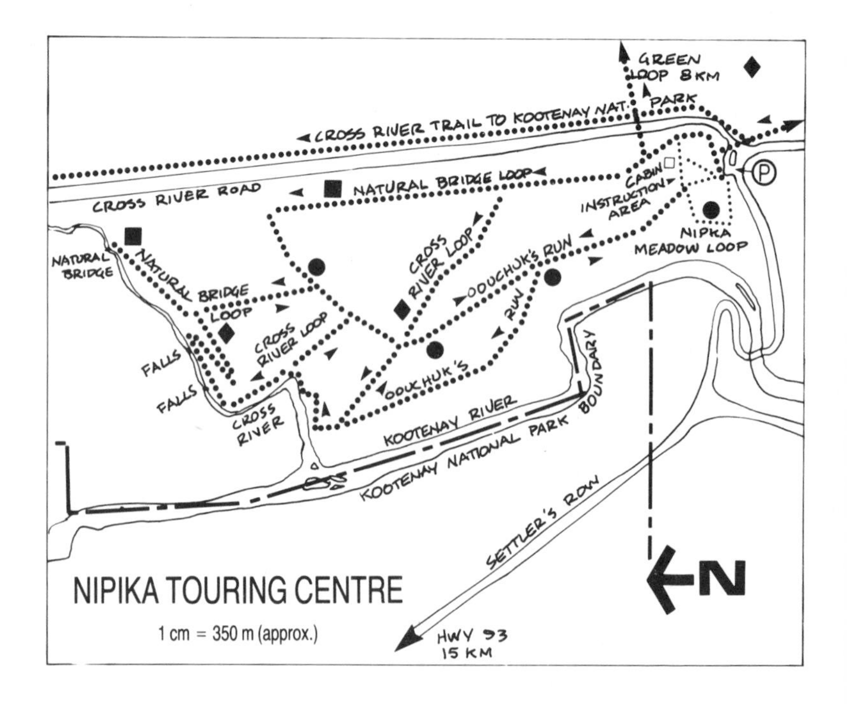

DIRECTIONS

The trails are located between Radium and Edgewater and may be reached by driving 9 km north from Radium on Highway 95 and turning right on Hewitt Road. Travel 3 km to the end of the road and follow signs.

DESCRIPTION

This system often changes depending on tree farm roads, but the trails are marked. Those on the lower slopes are generally best for beginners while intermediates can climb a little higher. Check at sporting goods stores in Radium for more information.

NIPIKA TOURING CENTRE

Level of Difficulty: Beginner to Advanced
Base Elevation: 1100 m
Length: 20-km network
Nearest Community: Radium Hot Springs, 23 km
Camping or Accommodations: Camping or primitive accommodations at Nipika; Radium Hot Springs
Map: Trail map available from Nipika Touring Centre, P.O. Box 903, Invermere, B.C. V0A 1K0, (604) 342-3130; trails are also shown on Outdoor Recreation Council Map #2, Windermere Lake Region

DIRECTIONS

From Radium drive north 14 km on Highway 93 to Settlers Road. The centre is at Mile 9 on this road. Watch for logging trucks.

DESCRIPTION

Nipika is the Kootenay Indian word for "Great Spirit." The centre actually operates at two locations, here and at Panorama Ski Resort near Invermere. At this location there are 20 km of looped, well-maintained trails near the confluence of the Cross and Kootenay rivers. Accommodations, instruction and guiding are available by reservation. This can also be the jumping off point for trails that lead into Kootenay National Park. See pp. 128, 129.

SKEENA REGION

The great tract of wilderness that is the Skeena Region is sparsely populated, with only a few small communities near the roads. Cross-country skiing is mostly done along logging roads and in river valleys near the towns along the Yellowhead Highway, from November to May.

GRANISLE SKI TRAILS

Level of Difficulty: Beginner to Intermediate
Base Elevation: 750 m
Nearest Community: All trails are near Granisle
Camping or Accommodations: Limited accommodations at Granisle
Map: Trail map available from the Granisle recreation office

DIRECTIONS

Granisle is 48 km north of Highway 16 at Topley.

DESCRIPTION

Granisle is a town built to service Granisle Copper and Noranda Mines. Located on Babine Lake, B.C.'s largest natural lake, it is the centre of much winter activity. A system of hiking trails has been developed which in winter are used for cross-country skiing. Trails begin in town and from various other points shown on the map. They cover a variety of terrain and in some cases lead to longer trails suitable for day touring.

As well as these cleared trails, many roads in the area, when unplowed, offer good touring.

HUDSON BAY MOUNTAIN

Level of Difficulty: Intermediate
Base Elevation: 1525 m
Nearest Community: Smithers, 24 km
Camping or Accommodations: Smithers
Map: Topographical map 1:250 000 available from Ministry of Environment, Surveys and Resource Mapping Branch

DIRECTIONS

Take King Street in Smithers southwest to Railway Avenue and then southeast to the railway crossing; follow Hudson Bay Mountain Road to the Prairie Ski Area road which leads up to the 1525-m level.

DESCRIPTION

The Hudson Bay Mountain plateau prairie area is popular with both downhill and cross-country skiers. There are open slopes above the timber line for the ski tourer, with magnificent views of the country below. The skiing season stretches from early November to mid-May. Cross-country skiers can ride free up the main hill on the T-bar.

The Smithers Ski Club has an annual ski tournament, usually on a weekend in March, which includes cross-country events.

A day lodge on the mountain has a ski shop and cafeteria.

TOBOGGAN CREEK

Level of Difficulty: Intermediate
Base Elevation: 600 m
Return Length: 19.2 km
Vertical Drop: 700 m
Nearest Community: Smithers, 12 km
Camping or Accommodations: Smithers
Map: Topographical map 1:250 000 available from Ministry of Environment, Surveys and Resource Mapping Branch

DIRECTIONS

Take Highway 16 west from Smithers 7 km to Lake Kathlyn Road; follow it 2.4 km and fork left on Glacier Gulch Road; approximately 2.4 km along this road is the beginning of the trail.

DESCRIPTION

The trail goes northwest, crossing Glacier Gulch Creek, until it reaches and follows Toboggan Creek, ascending the valley in a westerly direction. This route provides access to Silvern Lakes and is part of a possible route around Hudson Bay Mountain.

MOUNT HAYS

Mount Hays is the downhill ski area just outside Prince Rupert. There are 26 km of marked and groomed trails for cross-country skiers on this mountain. Take the gondola up Mount Hays to reach the trails. There is no charge for the trails but a gondola lift ticket must be purchased.

OMINECA-PEACE REGION

Most of this region is uninhabited. Areas for skiing are around Prince George and along the highways north and east of the city. The climate is fairly harsh and winters are long. Skiing can be done from late October to early May.

MOUNT ROBSON PROVINCIAL PARK

Base Elevation: 950 m
Nearest Communities: Jasper, 69 km east; Valemount, 53 km west and south
Camping or Accommodations: Park campsites closed in winter but campers can stay in Kinney Lake parking lot; motels in Jasper and Valemount
Map: Park brochure available from Ministry of Lands, Parks and Housing, Parks and Outdoor Recreation Division

DIRECTIONS

Mount Robson Provincial Park on the British Columbia–Alberta border can be reached by travelling east on Highway 16 from Prince George or north on Highway 5 from Kamloops.

DESCRIPTION

Mount Robson Provincial Park is named for the mountain towering above the Yellowhead Highway, the highest peak in the Canadian Rockies. The areas suitable for ski touring in this rugged mountain park centre around the lakes.

Anyone planning to camp in the park must have good winter camping equipment and should realize that the temperature can drop to $\pm 34°$ C. Skiers planning to be out overnight in the backcountry should notify the park administration at Red Pass. Also, there is a telephone at Red Pass.

Robson Park is a good place to watch for wildlife in the wintertime. Moose can frequently be seen; they sometimes use the relatively snow-free railway tracks for easy travelling. Also watch for coyotes and wolves. We have observed the wolves on Yellowhead Lake and have seen great grey owls near the lake.

KINNEY LAKE TRAIL

Level of Difficulty: Intermediate
Return length: 13 km
Vertical Drop: 170 m

Kinney Lake lies at the base of Mount Robson at a point 6.4 km along the Berg Lake hiking trail. Access is from the 2.4-km road leading north from Highway 16 at the Mount Robson Lookout. The parking lot at the trail head is kept open in winter. The trail itself winds up the Robson River valley and is groomed by the Parks Branch. Although the trail in summer continues to Berg Lake, in winter it passes through high-risk avalanche areas and must be checked out with the Parks Branch. There are cooking shelters at Kinney Lake and Berg Lake.

YELLOWHEAD LAKE

Level of Difficulty: Beginner
Return Length: Approximately 9 km
Vertical Drop: Negligible

Yellowhead Lake lies on the north side of the highway with Yellowhead Mountain (formerly the Seven Sisters) for a backdrop. The skier can make a loop of any length on the lake as there are no groomed trails yet.

MOOSE LAKE

Level of Difficulty: Beginner
Return Length: Variable
Vertical Drop: Negligible

The special attraction of Moose Lake and the marsh at its eastern end is the moose which are frequently seen in the area in winter. Moose Lake is about 8 km west of the Mount Robson Lookout parking lot, just off Highway 16.

RAVEN LAKE RECREATIONAL AREA

Level of Difficulty: Trail from Hungary Creek access at 13 km to Grizzly Den Cabin is suitable for beginners; others are more difficult
Return Length: Hungary Creek access at 13 km—5 km; Hungary Creek access at 15 km—4 km; Tumuch Road access—10 km
Vertical Drop: Approximately 610 m to Grizzly Den Cabin; 760 m to Raven Peak
Camping or Accommodations: Grizzly Den Cabin and Raven Lake Cabin, each sleeping 20, open to the public at no charge (Grizzly Den Cabin has an oil heater); Purden Lake Resort, 32 km west
Map: Trail map available from Northwood Pulp and Timber Ltd., P.O. Box 9000, Prince George, B.C. V2L 4W2; *also* N.T.S. map 1:50 000

DIRECTIONS

Follow Highway 16 east of Prince George to Hungary Creek Road, approximately 89 km east from the old Fraser Bridge. Go south on Hungary Creek Road 13 km to the first access point. A second access point is at 15 km on the same road. The third access is down the Bowron Access Road (70 km east of the old Fraser Bridge in Prince George) 60 km to Tumuch Road and along Tumuch Road 10 km.

DESCRIPTION

The trail from Hungary Creek access at 13 km crosses Hungary Creek and winds up the west ridge. Then it drops into a basin, and ascends to timber line where the A-frame Grizzly Den Cabin is located.

From the cabin the trail heads northwest through the basin between

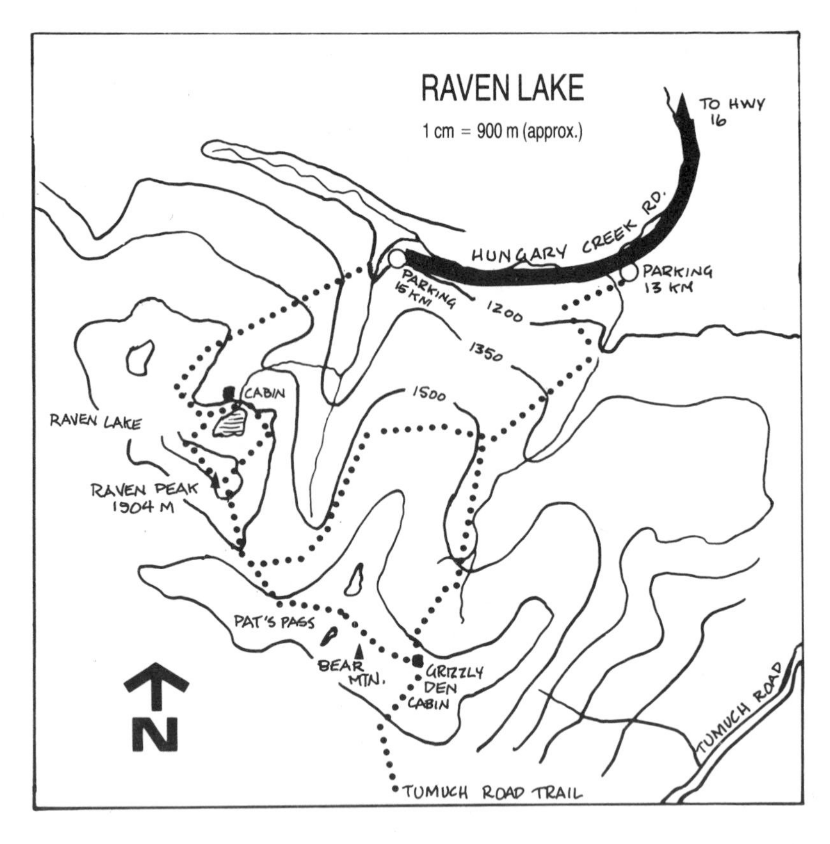

Bear Mountain and Raven Peak, then follows the toe of the ridge and proceeds up it to Raven Peak. The trail then ascends to a cabin by Raven Lake. (Both cabins are provided courtesy of Northwood Pulp and Timber.) The route from here follows the timber line and then goes northeast, dropping fairly quickly and ending at the second access point on Hungary Creek.

The Tumuch access road joins the other trails at Grizzly Den Cabin. There is some avalanche hazard on the trail from Tumuch Road. Also, the weather in this area is often unpredictable.

The Raven Lake Recreational Area provides a combination of wooded and alpine terrain. It is caribou and grizzly country, which should be a caution as well as an attraction.

TABOR MOUNTAIN RECREATIONAL RESERVE NETWORK

Level of Difficulty: Beginner to Advanced
Length: 3 km to 16 km; 50 km to 60 km total; some loop trails
Vertical Drop: 60 m to 400 m
Camping or Accommodations: Troll Lake Cabin and Tree Line Cabin, open to the public at no charge; Prince George
Map: Available from Sons of Norway Lodge, P.O. Box 772, Prince George, B.C. V2L 4T3

DIRECTIONS

Take Highway 16 east from Prince George. Approximately 13 km from the old Fraser Bridge is the start of the trail system at Sons of Norway Lodge on Tabor Lake (Six Mile Lake). About 9 km farther is the Tabor Mountain Ski Resort and the starting point for the Hickory Wing Ski Club X-Country Trails.

DESCRIPTION

The Recreational Reserve is being developed for skiers and hikers by sports groups from Prince George. The Sons of Norway have opened up ski trails over some of the old logging roads in the area. The Sons of Norway Lodge also has two cabins on the mountain open to the public.

About fifteen years ago a forest fire burned out of control on Tabor Mountain for twenty-two days. Many of the trails are located in the old burn area; some are in partially logged areas and a few in a virgin stand of timber. Occasionally moose or bears may be seen in the area.

Some of the main trails are as follows:

Circle Trail—loops at the toe of the mountain.
Crossover Trail—joins the Lookout Access Road and the D.O.T. Access Road about halfway up the west slope.
Hickory Wing Trail—begins on the upper slopes of Tabor and goes in a northeast direction down the mountain to the Hickory Wing ski area.
Highway 16 Trail—leads from the upper slopes of Tabor about 16 km to a point on Highway 16 between Tabor Ski Hill and Willow River.
Hydro Line Trail—follows the clearing between the peaks of Tabor Minor and Tabor Major.
Lookout Trail—goes down the north slope of Tabor Major.
Tabor Minor Trail—runs southeast from the toe of Tabor Major to the D.O.T. road on the south side of Tabor Minor.

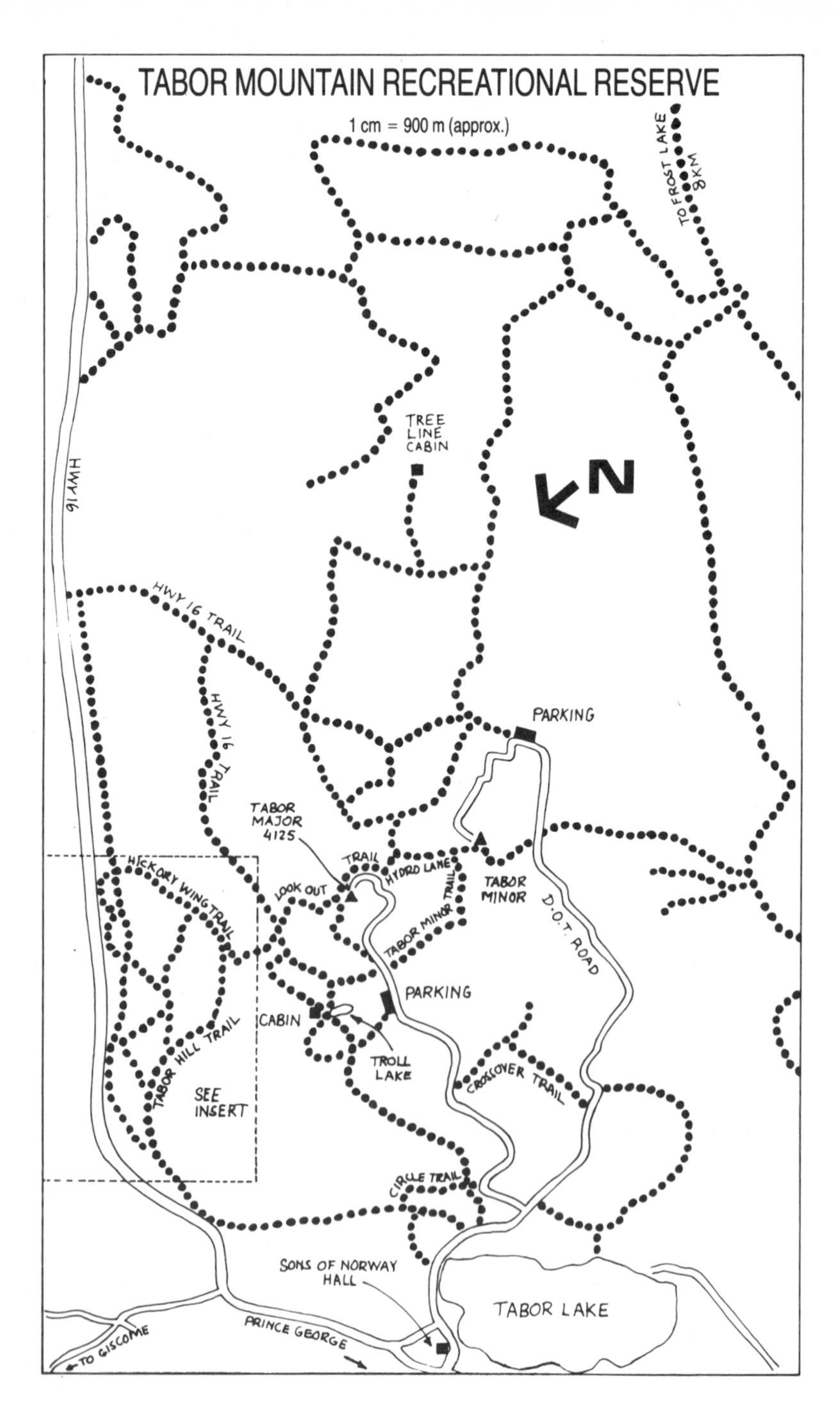
TABOR MOUNTAIN RECREATIONAL RESERVE
1 cm = 900 m (approx.)
TO FROST LAKE 8KM
TREE LINE CABIN
N
HWY 16
HWY 16 TRAIL
HWY 16 TRAIL
PARKING
TABOR MAJOR 4125
TRAIL
HYDRO LAKE
LOOK OUT
TABOR MINOR TRAIL
TABOR MINOR
HICKORY WING TRAIL
D.O.T. ROAD
PARKING
CABIN
TABOR HILL TRAIL
TROLL LAKE
CROSSOVER TRAIL
SEE INSERT
CIRCLE TRAIL
SONS OF NORWAY HALL
TABOR LAKE
PRINCE GEORGE
TO GISCOME

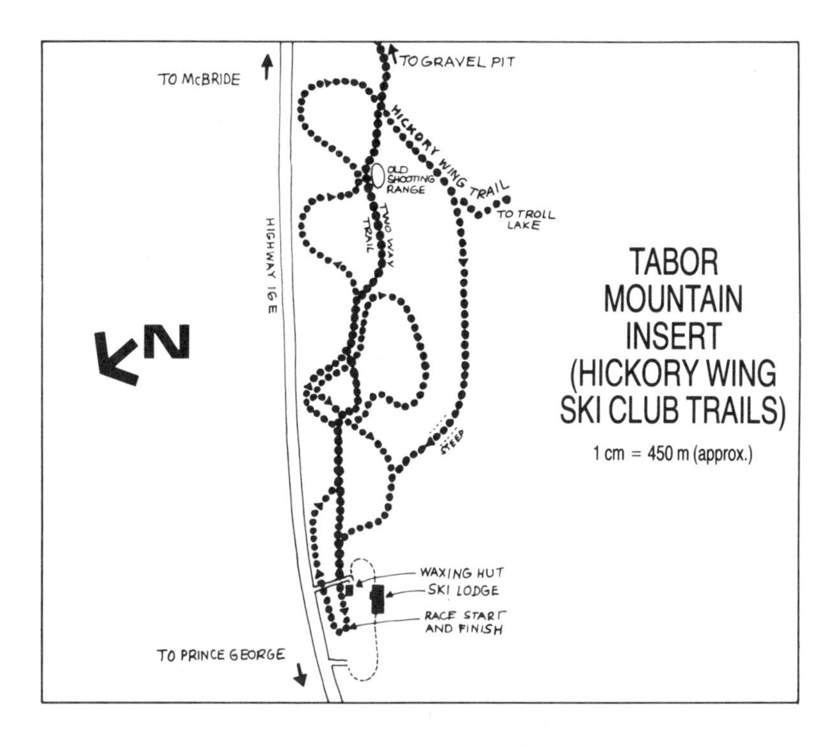

Tabor Trail—links up the entire area from north to south on the east side of Tabor Mountain; joins the Highway 16 trail to extend 40 km south to Buckhorn Road.

Tree Line Cabin Trail—leaves the parking area at the D.O.T. installation, goes east 3 km, then north 1 km, and east again up the hill to the cabin. The trail is cut and marked.

Troll Lake Trail—goes from the west toe of the mountain up to a ski cabin at Troll Lake.

On the north slope of the mountain is a network of five connecting trails from 2.5 km to 23.5 km that have been constructed, maintained and groomed by the Hickory Wing Ski Club of Prince George. The trails are all directional and are to be skied in clockwise direction. There is a map at the trail head. Also in the area is the Tabor Mountain Ski Resort where cross-country equipment rentals are available and where there are downhill facilities and a day lodge.

CROOKED RIVER PROVINCIAL PARK

Level of Difficulty: Beginner to Intermediate
Base Elevation: 760 m
Length: 25-km network
Vertical Drop: 90 m
Nearest Community: Prince George, 72 km
Camping or Accommodations: Winter camping for recreational vehicles in the parking lot of the park; Prince George
Map: Winter Recreation Park Brochure available from Ministry of Lands, Parks and Housing, Parks and Outdoor Recreation Division

DIRECTIONS

Follow Highway 97 (Hart Highway) 72 km north from Prince George.

DESCRIPTION

The Crooked River played an important part in the history of British Columbia. It was a route used by the Indians of the area and was later travelled by fur traders, and explorers such as Alexander Mackenzie and Simon Fraser. The marked ski trails in the park follow the summer hiking trails and are extended to cover areas too marshy for hiking. Six marked trails crisscross the park. The individual trails to Squaw Lake,

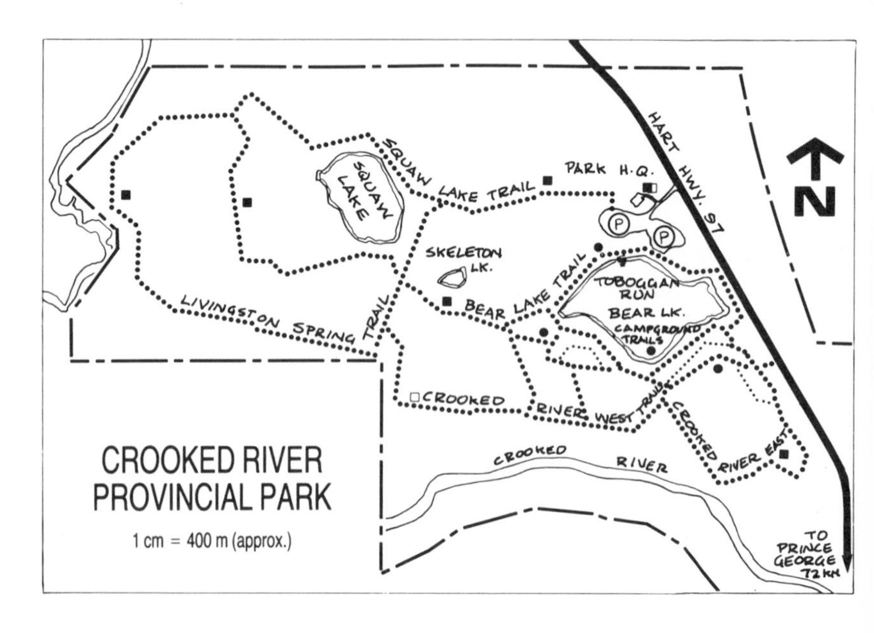

Bear Lake and Crooked River join up and make a good day trip, or they can be taken on their own. The campground roads make suitable Beginner trails. Other winter activities in the park include snowshoeing, ice fishing and tobogganing.

Watch for animal tracks in the snow and for animals such as moose and coyotes along the river. Trumpeter swans can sometimes be seen on the river in winter.

Trails in the park are as follows:

Bear Lake Trail, Beginner, 2.4 km return.
Campground Trail, Beginner, 3.2 km return.
Crooked River Trail (east), Intermediate, 2.4 km return, 40 m vertical drop.
Crooked River Trail (west), Intermediate, 5.6 km return, 90 m vertical drop.
Livingston Springs Trail, Intermediate, 4.8 km return.
Squaw Lake Trail, Intermediate, 7.2 km return.

APPENDIX 1

CROSS-COUNTRY SKI CONTACTS

For information on cross-country skiing, contact the following organizations or departments:

B.C. Ski Association
1200 Hornby Street
Vancouver, B.C. V6Z 1W2
Phone: (604) 687-6028
(Ski race information)

Canadian Association Nordic Ski Instructors (CANSI)
1200 Hornby Street
Vancouver, B.C. V6Z 1W2
Phone: (604) 387-5985
(Ski instructions and instructor qualifications)

Information Services Branch
Ministry of Forests
Parliament Buildings
Victoria, B.C. V8V 1X4
Phone: (604) 387-5985

Outdoor Recreation Council
1200 Hornby Street
Vancouver, B.C. V6Z 2E2
Phone: (604) 687-3333
(Safety and trail information)

Outdoor Recreation Department
Capilano College
2055 Purcell Way
North Vancouver, B.C. V7J 3H5
Phone: (604) 986-1911
(Winter survival courses)

Parks and Outdoor Recreation Division,
South Coast Region
Ministry of Lands, Parks and Housing
1610 Indian River Drive
North Vancouver, B.C. V7G 1L3
(Park brochures)

Survey and Resource Mapping Branch
Ministry of Environment
Victoria, B.C. V5V 1X5
(maps)

National Topographic Series (N.T.S.) maps
can be obtained from:
Geological Survey of Canada
100 West Pender Street
Vancouver, B.C. V6B 1R8

APPENDIX 2

WINTER DRIVING

Not everyone who enjoys cross-country skiing is fortunate to be able to ski from their own front door. For the majority of people it is necessary to drive in winter conditions to get to the ski area and this may involve travelling on back roads. It is wise to keep a few precautions in mind.

— Your car should have a complete winter checkup with special emphasis on heater, antifreeze, exhaust system, battery and fuel systems.
— Carry an emergency storm kit with matches, blankets or sleeping bags, map, compass, extra food, first aid kit, knife, shovel, sand or salt, signal light or flares, and chains. A small stove or a thermos (preferably filled) would also be handy.
— Listen to weather reports and watch the sky. If a severe storm comes, seek shelter.
— Select an alternative route where possible, particularly if you have mountain passes to cross.
— Be cautious about taking back roads.
— On little-travelled routes consider a small convoy.

If you become stranded:

— Don't struggle too hard to free your car.
— Stay in the vehicle or you may become lost.
— Guard against carbon monoxide poisoning and lack of oxygen.
— Run the engine and heater sparingly to conserve fuel, and keep a downwind window partly open. Freezing temperatures and blowing, drifting snow can seal a vehicle airtight.
— Move around frequently. Try doing exercises to keep circulation up.
— Keep a light burning at night so rescue or highway crews can find you.
— Have someone watching for help at all times.

APPENDIX 3

THE OUTDOOR CAMERA IN WINTER

To nonskiers, or people who do not know the enjoyment of snow and cold, a camera is something to be used in the summer, and stored away in winter. That should not be the case with cross-country skiers. Winter is a good time for photos, a time to add some variety to your photography, a time to record those events and friends about which you build memories.

Except for a few peculiar problems, winter photography is not very different from any other type of photography. With an understanding of these few peculiarities your camera should see as much use at –20° as it does at +20°. Pictures of people, action, nature close-up, wildlife, scenery and camping should not be confined to warm weather. Let's look at a few critical areas: equipment, film and exposure.

Equipment

Just as extremely hot weather requires certain precautions, so does extreme cold. Fortunately, modern cameras require fewer precautions than they did a few years ago when it was common to have cameras "winterized." The lubricants in cameras and lenses are designed for operation at moderate temperatures, and anyone who has tried to start a car on a very cold morning knows that when lubricants get cold they thicken up. In cameras this can mean that a lens is hard to focus, stiff to turn. Lens diaphragms may also become stiff and stick at certain apertures. The shutter may slow down, or stick closed or open. Also, a mirror on a single lens reflex may freeze up, or crystals of ice or snow may embed themselves in the same manner as grains of sand in a focussing mount.

Should any of these problems occur while you are skiing it is usually sufficient to place your camera where you would a frost-bitten limb, although you may want a little covering between the two surfaces. If you are curious to see how your camera will react to cold, place it in your freezer for a time and see how it operates upon removal.

All of this may make it sound as if a camera should, after all, be left at home. Not so! First of all, these problems do not usually occur except in extreme conditions, and with most modern cameras the tolerances and more refined lubricants alleviate the situation. However, if you are planning a trip to the Arctic, the top of Mount Logan or a long winter camp, you might want to consider having your camera winterized. The cost is considerable as all the lubricants have to be replaced with thinner viscosities, and then changed back again when you return to a temperate climate.

When actually skiing or camping in winter you can do a number of things to avoid the problems mentioned.

Remember that while carrying cases protect the camera from snow, rain or blows, they will also prevent you from grab shooting, and if a case is difficult to open in the summer it will be worse when your hands are wrapped in wool or stiff with cold. Whether in a case or not, the camera should be kept inside your sweater or jacket, worn on a wide neck strap. This keeps it both warm and protected. Of course, if you fall forward you may have the imprint of a camera back on your front!

We prefer to carry ours without a case on a wide strap with an additional elastic strap around our front, but should the weather turn bad or the trail become at all difficult, we use a case, swung to a position under one arm near the back. The position you choose will depend on how you ski, on whether you want to take photos quickly, on whether you use a case, and on the type of camera. Extra gear such as spare film, meter, lenses, filters, even a few tissues for drying the camera, are carried in a fanny pack which can be easily swung to the front for equipment or film changing.

A few other cautions are in order for winter equipment care. Do not try to blow snow or dust off your camera lenses when outside—your breath may condense on the surface and freeze; this "frost" is difficult to remove and will make your photos very diffused. A cold camera brought indoors, whether into a cabin, warm tent or car, will tend to have moisture condense on it. This may be avoided by placing it in a plastic bag while still cold, and allowing it to warm gradually to room temperature. Particles of snow or ice should be blown off before they have a chance to melt.

The batteries that run your camera, meter or flash unit are also affected by cold. In very cold weather batteries may lose all their power, resulting in a nonfunctioning camera, a meter that grossly overexposes photos, or a flash unit that does not have enough power to light a scene. Some of these failures may not be apparent to you. Check your batteries, and keep them warm.

Film

Like camera equipment, film too can be adversely affected by low temperatures and moisture. The most frequent problem with film occurs with thick emulsion film, "faster" films such as those around 400 ASA. The thickness of the film makes it less flexible and therefore stiffer in the cold, and more susceptible to breakage. It is not uncommon to have such film become brittle and break (even around freezing), particularly when loading and trying to wrap it around the take-up spool for the first time. The only remedy is to keep the film warm (not hot). Treat it gently and evenly, or use another film. Slower speed colour films do not usually have this problem.

The choice of a film for winter photography must take a number of situations and problems into account. Generally the light in winter is much brighter with more contrast than in summer. That is on a fine day! The rest of the time the whole landscape tends to merge into a soft dull grey tone. What is needed is a low contrast slow film. Unfortunately, slow films have higher contrast in either colour or black and white. Kodak's Tri X 400 ASA—a fast film—has a good contrast range for fine weather conditions, but it is too fast unless you want to use neutral density filters to cut the light down. At the other end of the scale are slow films well balanced to the amount of light, but high in contrast. In black and white there is really no easy solution. A good choice would be Panatomic X ASA 32, a fine grain film with medium contrast. On dull days try Plus X ASA 125, with increased contrast and speed, or Tri X if the light is poor.

In colour film the same problems occur but the range of choice is smaller. Kodachromes are more contrasty than, say, an Ektachrome, but the brilliant snow whites, deep blues of the sky and bright ski clothing are strikingly reproduced on these films: either Kodachrome 25 or 64. Ektachrome might be tried for a softer tone, particularly for greens and sometimes blues, and of course High Speed Ektachrome if the weather is poor or you are photographing action and need a faster shutter speed.

Experimentation is the best way to arrive at the film that suits you.

Exposure

If there is one problem with winter photography that encourages questions from students and would-be photographers, and discourages others from trying at all, it is exposure. The concern is a real one, and a constant problem, but it need not be if you are willing to do a little practice with your camera and a couple of rolls of film, and if you have a basic understanding of how and why a light meter works.

All cameras equipped with meters have what is called a *reflected light meter*. This means that it reads the light *reflected from* a subject, rather than the light *falling on* a subject. A meter designed to read light falling on a subject is called an *incident light meter*.

When a reflected light meter reads the light intensity of a scene it interprets everything in the scene in such a way as to make it appear as a middle grey in the resulting photo. This grey is represented by a Kodak Gray Card—one that has a reflectance of 18 percent. This is the average reflectance of most subjects. It means, though, that if you were to meter and separately photograph a black card, a grey card, and a white card, each would be reproduced as a tone with 18-percent reflectance. They would all appear grey. This is because your reflected light meter would have indicated a different exposure for each photo and card, based on its reflectance. In this case of course the reflectance was extreme in the case of both the white and the black. Had the meter you used been an *incident meter* it would have read the light *falling on* the subject, which was the same for each card. Then the black would be black, and white would be white. A third alternative would have been to use a reflected meter, but not let it decide for you what the exposure would be; that is, use it to give you a "base," and then adjust the exposure according to your own experience.

Now, how does all this relate to winter photography? In the first place most winter scenes do not have a reflectance of 18 percent; in fact it is up to 85 percent on bright days. And most cameras are equipped with reflected light meters that give an exposure reading based on this reflectance. If you think of the white card example as snow you will see that your snow will turn out grey. And chances are you do not want grey snow. To avoid this there a number of courses of action.

You could purchase an *incident meter,* one that will probably also take *reflected readings* but will have a "hemisphere" of white plastic that slides over the meter cell for *incident readings*. This is the best and most accurate solution, and will result in the best winter photos. Now you will read the light falling on your subject, on the snow or the black forest, and your exposure will be more accurate. This, of course, means using a hand-held meter. Often, though, you will be able to take a couple of readings and only change your basic exposure when you move into shade or when a cloud passes over.

You don't want to buy another meter? If your camera is one that takes "spot" reflected readings you probably won't have the problem, for you

can, and probably will, take the readings from a subject other than snow. Even with a normal meter you can do this. Purchase an 18-percent grey card and carry it with you, or learn some of the things that have the same reflectance. Take your reading from these subjects, *not* the one to be photographed. Some examples are: green grass (difficult to find under the snow); the palm of a Caucasian hand (about one stop *over* an 18-percent grey, i.e. you should *open up one stop*); perhaps your pack or parka, a ski or your knickers. By buying a card and comparing readings with other subjects you can easily find some things to meter from.

Practice should tell you how much your exposures are, particularly if you "bracket" them for a couple of shots—that is, take an extra shot on either side of the correct exposure. If the meter reads f8 try one shot at f5.6 and one at f11. You will probably find that you are one to two stops underexposed on a sunny day on snow. That is, your reflected meter will read f16 instead of f8. So from then on you can mentally adjust accordingly, a common practice in all exposure readings. A meter cannot translate the quality of the light nor interpret what it is you want to show.

Finally, you could shoot some tests and adjust your ASA setting to "fool" the meter. For instance, if your ASA is 100 and the meter is always reading f16 on snow instead of f8, then set the ASA setting for 25. This will make the meter "open up" the two stops to accommodate the higher reflectance. Practice! That is really the only way to be sure of good exposures in such conditions.

The outdoor camera will not only bring back memories for you, but it will, if you allow it, open your eyes and mind to the wonders of the winter landscape as only a cross-country skier can experience it. You have presumably chosen this sport for its closeness to nature, its relatively slow pace and other personal reasons. A camera fits well with these desires, and in fact will allow you to enjoy them more fully.

SUGGESTED READING LIST

Baldwin, Ned. *Skiing Cross Country*. Toronto: McGraw-Hill Ryerson, 1977.

Barnett, Steve. *Cross-Country Downhill*. Seattle: Pacific Search Press, 1979.

Barz, Don, et al. *Trails to the Shuswap*. Salmon Arm: Shuswap Outdoors, 1976.

Blix, Einar. *Trails to Timberline in West Central B.C.* Terrace: Northern Times Press, 1977.

Brady, M. Michael. *Nordic Touring and Cross Country Skiing*. New York: Port City Press, 1975.

Bridge, Raymond. *The Complete Snow Camper's Guide*. New York: Charles Scribner's Sons, 1973.

British Columbia. Department of Recreation and Conservation. *Beware of Hypothermia*. Pamphlet.

———. *British Columbia Recreational Atlas*. Victoria: Ministry of Environment, 1981.

Bus, K. Ben. *Waxing and Cross Country Technique*. Edmonton: Whistler Publishing, 1978.

Caldwell, John. *Cross Country Skiing Today*. Brattleboro, Vt.: The Stephen Greene Press, 1977.

Daffern, Tony and Gillean. *Kananaskis Country*. Calgary: Rocky Mountain Books, 1979.

Fear, Gene. *Surviving the Unexpected Wilderness Emergency*. Tacoma: Survival Education Association, 1975.

Kirk, Ruth. *Snow*. New York: William Morrow & Co., 1978.

Kunelius, Rick, and Biederman, Dave. *Ski Trails in the Canadian Rockies*. Banff: Summerthought, 1981.

LaChappelle, Edward R. *Field Guide to Snow Crystals*. Seattle: University of Washington Press, 1980.

———. *The ABC of Avalanche Safety*. Seattle: The Mountaineers, 1978.

McDonald, Monique. *Cross-Country Skiing at Whistler Mountain*. Alta Lake Sports Club, 1976.

Mitchell, Richard. *Mountaineering First Aid*. 4th ed. Seattle: The Mountaineers, 1978.

Nelson, Bob. *The Prince George and District Trail Guide*. Prince George: Caledonia Ramblers, 1978.

Outdoor Recreation Council of B.C. *Cross-Country Skiing: A Guide to Safety in British Columbia*. Pamphlet.

Peters, Ed, ed. *Mountaineering: The Freedom of the Hills*. 4th ed. Vancouver: Douglas & McIntyre, 1982.

Watters, Ron. *Ski Camping*. Vancouver: Douglas & McIntyre, 1979.

Magazines for Reference

BC Outdoors. #202 - 1132 Hamilton Street, Vancouver, B.C. V6B 2S2

Explore. P.O. Box 4014, Station C, Calgary, Alta. T2T 5M9

Outside. Continental Bank Building, 1165 North Clark Street, Chicago, Ill. 60610

Ski Canada. 425 University Avenue, Toronto, Ont. M5S 1T6

Western Living. #303 - 2930 Arbutus Street, Vancouver, B.C. V6J 3Y9

INDEX